Barnes & Noble Shakespeare

David Scott Kastan
Series Editor

BARNES & NOBLE SHAKESPEARE features newly edited texts of the plays prepared by the world's premiere Shakespeare scholars. Each edition provides new scholarship with an introduction, commentary, unusually full and informative notes, an account of the play as it would have been performed in Shakespeare's theaters, and an essay on how to read Shakespeare's language.

DAVID SCOTT KASTAN is the Old Dominion Foundation Professor in the Humanities at Columbia University and one of the world's leading authorities on Shakespeare.

Barnes & Noble Shakespeare
Published by Barnes & Noble
122 Fifth Avenue
New York, NY 10011
www.barnesandnoble.com/shakespeare

Image on page 298:
William Shakespeare, *Comedies, Histories, & Tragedies*, London, 1623, Bequest of Stephen Whitney Phoenix, Rare Book & Manuscript Library, Columbia University.

Library of Congress Cataloging-in-Publication Data

Shakespeare, William, 1564–1616.
Taming of the shrew / William Shakespeare.
    p. cm. — (Barnes & Noble Shakespeare)
Includes bibliographical references.
ISBN-13: 978-1-4114-0041-2
ISBN-10: 1-4114-0041-0
1. Man-woman relationships—Drama. 2. Married people—Drama. 3. Padua (Italy)—Drama. 4. Sex role—Drama. I. Title.

PR2832.A1 2006
822.3'3—dc22   2006018626

Printed and bound in the United States
1 3 5 7 9 10 8 6 4 2

THE TAMING OF THE SHREW

William SHAKESPEARE

NICHOLAS F. RADEL

EDITOR

Barnes & Noble Shakespeare

Contents

Introduction to *The Taming of the Shrew*
by Nicholas F. Radel

lthough it remains popular both in the study and on the stage, *The Taming of the Shrew* is one of Shakespeare's most troubling comedies. The story of how a supposed shrew, Katherina, is transformed into a docile and obedient wife by her husband Petruchio, voices attitudes about gender and women's roles in marriage that seem outdated at best, brutal and offensive at worst. Women in the play are represented as potentially disorderly and lacking self-control. Even though the word "shrew" could apply to both men and women in early modern London, here the men in the play and in fact the play itself (by way of its title) use it to describe women who talk too much or challenge male authority. The word registers the extraordinary anxiety men in Shakespeare's period may have felt about women like Katherina, who stepped out of line or failed to know their place in the hierarchy of men and women that was assumed at the time the play was written in the early 1590s. By the end of the play, Petruchio's successful "taming" of the shrew is made clear in Katherina's final speech, which justifies marriage as a feudal, hierarchical arrangement in which women take a subordinate position to men:

> Such duty as the subject owes the prince,
> Even such a woman oweth to her husband.

And when she is froward, peevish, sullen, sour,
And not obedient to his honest will,
What is she but a foul contending rebel
And graceless traitor to her loving lord?   (5.2.165–170)

Defining marriage in ways that run contrary to our usual expectations about the relations between husbands and wives, Katherina reflects and elaborates the words of her husband, who says to the other men in the play that Katherina's transformation bodes "peace . . . and love, and quiet life, / An awful rule, and right supremacy" (5.2.118–119). We might very well ask what we are to make of such a play.

And we might answer in one of two ways, either referring to the play's genre or to differences in the historical understanding of marriage from Shakespeare's time to our own. As a comedy, *The Taming of the Shrew* encourages us to see its ending as a benevolent conclusion to a disorderly social world. What makes Shakespeare's play different from other versions of the popular tale about taming a wife is that Petruchio uses no physical violence against Katherina, and although his methods hardly seem enlightened from a modern standpoint, many people have seen him as providing a legitimate alternative for Katherina, whose family situation at the beginning of the play is, in itself, somewhat abusive: her father, Baptista, for instance, clearly seems to favor his younger daughter, Bianca. Where other men call Katherina "Kate the curst," Petruchio tells her she is the "prettiest Kate in Christendom" (2.1.186–187). He may have ulterior motives, but he seems to genuinely admire her spirit and wit, and, depending on how we interpret his subsequent actions, we might imagine Katherina prospering in marriage with a man she has learned to respect and love, a man who returns both. In Shakespeare's comedies, marriage often symbolizes the resolution of social problems and personal fruition in the promise of love and children.

Conversely, we might turn to history. Looked at this way, the play reveals a good deal about masculine prerogative and the social expectations that constrained women in Shakespeare's time. The vision of marriage that Katherina describes in her final speech describes an ideal of a society ordered (as Shakespeare's was) in hierarchical categories, and that ideal would have been widely corroborated by the pamphlet writers, moralists, and religious thinkers of the day. In *The Law's Resolution of Women's Rights* (1632), for instance, the author known only as T.E. says that a "wife how gallant soever she be, glistereth but in the riches of her husband, as the moon hath no light, but it is the sun's." This does not mean that women had no power or ability to speak on their own behalf. As we can see even in *The Shrew*, both Katherina and Bianca, as daughters of a rich merchant, have some leeway in controlling their lives and directing their servants. Their power is exercised, however, within the expectations of a social ideology of gender that placed women beneath men. Ultimately, women who failed to conform to male authority might come to be seen as serious social threats—as, to some extent, Katherina is.

In this respect, Petruchio's aggressive taming of Katherina and her capitulation to a masculine-centered hierarchy in marriage reflects dominant cultural fears that women would not fulfill their expected roles in the household and would not accept the authority that seems so naturally invested in men. It is no accident that Katherina's words appeal to perceived differences between women's "soft," "weak," and "smooth" bodies and men's tougher ones (5.2.175). Her speech naturalizes the cultural misogyny of the period, making it seem inevitable rather than what it is: a particular construction of masculine power and privilege.

But *The Taming of the Shrew* is a play; it is not a simple rehearsal of history. What makes it continue to be popular and compelling to playgoers and readers is not its antiquated vision of hierarchical family relations—as fascinating as that is in terms of historical understanding. Rather, it is Shakespeare's brilliant handling of character and the play's witty—if sometimes disquieting—revelation of the complexities of gender relations in the early modern period and perhaps in our own. There is no way to remove the stain of misogyny from the play. It is largely written from a male perspective, and, although Kate and Bianca seem to be its central characters, it is arguably as concerned with Petruchio's masculinity as it is with the gender roles available to and adopted by the two women. To the extent that it examines femininity, it does so within a narrow range that imagines only two models: shrew and wife. Nevertheless, the play chronicles the ways Katherina's supposed aggressions both challenge and enable Petruchio in his bid to become a man in his own right, and it suggests that masculinity may be seen as an almost paranoid reaction to the fear of unruly women. For both the two sisters and Petruchio, gender is revealed to be a social role one learns to play, a language one learns to speak, and it is explored in *The Taming of the Shrew* in the complicated interplay between men and women.

When Petruchio arrives in Padua he is a young man in a precarious situation: his father has died and left him an estate. But he has no wife to help him manage it (in this regard, women were indispensable), and he has not yet proven himself with regard to other men. On his initial entrance, Petruchio is full of brag and bluster. When the men try to warn him about Katherina he responds in an absurdly comic way: "Have I not in my time heard lions roar? / Have I not heard the sea, puffed up with winds . . . / Have I not heard great ordnance in the field . . . ?" (1.2.196–199). It is speculation, of course, but the answer is probably no. Petruchio is a merchant's son. He is not an adventurer, sailor, or soldier. These boasts are empty words that affect a stereotypical pose of masculinity. They do not suggest the stability and assurance of command that comes with being a man in Shakespeare's England.

The great joke, of course, which the audience already knows, is that Petruchio will more than meet his match in Katherina. From the beginning, Shakespeare characterizes her as witty, fiery, and petulant, helping us see what seems to be most threatening to the men in the play: women do not always conform to male expectations, and they sometimes insist on speaking with independent resolve. Katherina in particular has an astonishing way with words, and she uses her skills with glee against the men who delight in insulting her. When Hortensio scornfully says she will get no husband until she behaves more mildly and gently, she responds with sly irony that translates into direct aggression:

> I' faith, sir, you shall never need to fear.
> Iwis it is not halfway to her heart,
> But if it were, doubt not her care should be
> To comb your noddle with a three-legged stool
> And paint your face and use you like a fool.   (1.1.61–65)

This kind of competitive, aggressive, even, we might say, "mannish," language contrasts Katherina with the ideally silent and modest woman Bianca plays at this point in the play. Yet it remains unclear whether the insults and provocations of the supposed gentlemen of Padua inspire Katherina's shrewishness or her anger begets their curses. One of the insights of the play may be that men's fear of women results from the clear evidence of independent self-determination that an intelligent woman like Katherina demonstrates.

As if to reinforce the point, Shakespeare shows that when Katherina meets Petruchio she seems to intuit his insecurities, and one aspect of the play that creates its great comic appeal is that she seems to sense and exploit this weakness. On their first meeting, when Petruchio says that he is "moved to woo" her for his wife, she twists his words to attack his masculinity: "I knew you at the first / You were a moveable" (2.1.194, 196–197). She literally means that he is a joint stool, something for "asses" to sit on, a scatological if not a sodomitical image (2.1.199). Less literally, she suggests that he is insecure, not firmly established, and hence not a man. Although his equally witty response reminds her that he does indeed have the equipment

necessary to be a man—"Thou hast hit it. Come sit on me" (2.1.198)—
it alludes directly to her palpable assault on his masculinity. The entire
scene of their first meeting unfolds in a similar excess of witty banter
that makes it a comic masterpiece 400 years after it was written, but
beneath the glittering verbal surface, the anxious interactions of men
and women are vividly dramatized.

As with Beatrice and Benedick in *Much Ado About Nothing*, harmony in wit and linguistic ability often distinguishes Shakespeare's
memorable romantic couples. But in this much earlier comedy, Shakespeare exploits the convention differently. Petruchio's identity as a
man depends not only on his wooing, taming, wedding, and bedding
Katherina, but on his controlling her will or desire by controlling her
use of words, her speech. Such control perhaps seems necessary in
the logic of the play because her enjoyment of word play and language
games reflects a similar love in him that is not entirely manly. In Shakespeare's plays, empty words were often associated with effeminate
men and cowards. So if Katherina's aggressive language marks her as
a shrew (a smart and savvy one to be sure), even in some senses "mannish," Petruchio's initial uses of language reveal him to be something
less than manly. Not only is he full of bluff that he has not so far corroborated, but he also seems to enjoy playing the kind of language
games associated with the seemingly unreasonable Katherina.

Early on, then, Katherina seems very powerful and her threat
very real, for her failure to speak in ways proper to her position both
menaces and enables Petruchio. On the one hand, she tempts him into
a perpetual play with words that he seems already drawn to, and on the
other she provides him the occasion to gain control of her language
and through that his own. It is a challenge to which he rises at the end
of their first scene together, when he cuts short the verbal play: "setting
all this chat aside . . . I am he am born to tame you, Kate" (2.1.261–269).

To be a man in Shakespeare's England meant in part that
one learned to control one's affections and emotions for women.

As opposed perhaps to our own time in which manhood is revealed through one's relation to women, in Shakespeare's it depended more on one's ability to remain distant from and in control of them. Petruchio must learn to control Katherina so that he will not be or remain feminized in his love for her. Thus his taming of her might be seen as an attempt to redirect her language toward more suitable "feminine" models, which, ironically, means ones controlled by him. Although he becomes more and more aggressive over the course of the play—removing Katherina from her home and denying her food and sleep, acts that in modern terms would signify abuse—the pivotal moment of his taming comes when he succeeds in controlling her language.

On the road back to her father's, Petruchio insists that Katherina call the sun the moon, and vice versa, according to his desire: "Now, by my mother's son, and that's myself, / It shall be moon, or star, or what I list" (4.5.6–7). The scene becomes a test of Katherina's willingness to follow Petruchio's lead in spite of what she may believe, and her resolve is put to the test immediately following when old Vincentio enters. Petruchio hails him as a fresh "gentlewoman," and Katherina replies, by this point seeming to understand the game Petruchio is playing, with "Young budding virgin, fair and fresh and sweet, / Whither away, or where is thy abode?" (4.5.30, 38–39). Ironically, Petruchio leads Katherina to perceive in Vincentio a feminine gender role that she herself (and indeed the play as a whole) lacks, and perhaps at this point Katherina gets the joke and goes along with it.

Significantly, she maintains the same vigor of language she had demonstrated formerly, only now it has been authorized by Petruchio. This moment, as much as any other in the play, marks the transition from shrew to wife. It is a linguistic moment in which the woman literally becomes one with her husband either by speaking his desire as her own or by coming to understand the mutuality of their interests. In order not to be one version of the female gender, a shrew, Katherina has to become another, a wife, and as we shall see it is a role that unites her with Petruchio by pitting her against the other women in the play. Indeed at the end of the play, as a condition of Petruchio's demonstrating his mastery over Katherina, he insists that she demonstrate her mastery of the other women by lecturing them. Not only does Petruchio authorize her words and consequently her desire, but he also seems to provide a vocabulary for her new-found role as the female who lectures other women. Katherina, then, reveals her new feminine identity as one that is not simply subordinate to men but separate from other women. Femininity in this sense is not a class that categorizes all women. It is something else altogether, something related to a husband, and the proper word for it is "wife."

Petruchio's masculinity, however, does not emerge simply from his control of his wife. It depends as well on his using his relationship with her to define a place for himself within a world of men who, at every moment, expect his failure. After his initial interview with Katherina, when he announces their wedding and she rebukes him, Gremio ridicules him: "Hark, Petruchio; she says she'll see thee hanged first" (2.1.293). While it is in Gremio's best interest for Petruchio to succeed, a significant tension exists between the two, no doubt based on the threat the young man poses to Gremio's age. It is a threat that symbolizes the trajectory of Petruchio's desire to become a man in his own right. So, after the wedding, when Petruchio resists all entreaties to stay for dinner, he addresses the men in a commanding tone that seems new to him. Katherina, he says,

> . . . is my goods, my chattels; she is my house,
> My household stuff, my field, my barn,
> My horse, my ox, my ass, my anything.
> And here she stands. Touch her whoever dare.
> I'll bring mine action on the proudest he
> That stops my way in Padua.   (3.2.226–231)

A good example of what his servant Grumio calls Petruchio's "rope tricks" (1.2.109), or rhetorical games, these lines pretend that the men are attempting to keep Katherina at the wedding feast against her will. But, more important, they warn the men not to expect his failure. His words will be proven no boast only in the contest that ends the play, when Petruchio defends the validity of his untraditional household within a conservative male world even as he defends its boundaries by controlling Katherina and her connection to other women.

In short, Petruchio's masculinity will be revealed most fully through his participation in and winning of the contest to determine who has the most obedient wife. As the contest at the end suggests, Petruchio wins not only Katherina but also the approbation of her father and the admiration of the other men in the play. Like a good comedy, the play ends in general wonder and amazement at Katherina's transformation and Petruchio's skill. But it is Baptista who reveals exactly what is at stake:

> Now, fair befall thee, good Petruchio!
> The wager thou hast won, and I will add
> Unto their losses twenty thousand crowns,
> Another dowry to another daughter,
> For she is changed as she had never been.   (5.2.121–125)

Baptista has gained a new daughter and a new son. Petruchio, who began the play disconnected from the paternal world by the death of his father, has gained a new place within that world of men. He merges the roles of father and husband that are implied by the orthodox, hierarchical vision of marriage Katherina articulates at the end.

This version of marriage and gender relations is not in any sense real, of course. It is a masculine fantasy—certainly Petruchio's and perhaps the author's as well—a point that might be corroborated by Shakespeare's handling of the subplot. As has been widely remarked,

Bianca only seems to be the good daughter in the play, and much of Katherina's supposed bad behavior seems to be provoked by Baptista's apparently greater love and caring for his younger daughter. Bianca shrewdly if not shrewishly negotiates between two lovers surreptitiously, and she ends up eloping with one of them without her father's knowledge or consent. The closer one looks at her, the slyer she seems, so that by the end of the play, when she calls her husband a fool, she seems to be as shrewish as her sister was formerly. Bianca comes to speak a language of resistance to male authority that had been previously associated with her sister. It is a trick of contrasts that the play depends on to justify Petruchio's taming of Katherina. Ostensibly Petruchio brings his wife to a place where happiness is possible for both of them, while happiness for Lucentio and Bianca seems to be up in the air because Lucentio cannot bring Bianca to a similar degree of conformity as Kate.

But it is of course possible to imagine Bianca in another way. When Lucentio calls for her in the contest at the end of the play, she answers that "she is busy, and she cannot come" (5.2.87). Such an answer could have been represented as a more reasonable response to the give and take of marriage than Lucentio, Petruchio, or even Katherina can imagine—as a language of mutual cooperation. Certainly that is an option imagined in Shakespeare's own lifetime in a sequel to his play by a younger friend and colleague, John Fletcher. In *The Woman's Prize; or The Tamer Tamed* (1611), Fletcher tells the story of Petruchio's second marriage. His new wife, Maria, believes that Katherina died an early death because of the damage done to her by Petruchio's taming. Instructed by Byancha (as Fletcher spells the name), Maria undertakes to reform her new husband—not by simply reversing the situation but by teaching him the value of compromise and restraint. Shakespeare's play, however, does not allow for such a solution even in its subplot, precisely because it represents the relationship of Bianca and Lucentio as inadequate and in contrast to the different types of gender roles that apparently make for a successful marriage in the main plot.

We might say that *The Taming of the Shrew* needs a shrew, and in this respect both Bianca and Hortensio's widow serve to suggest that while Katherina's subversive energies may be contained by her taming as a wife, that does not contain the threat apparently posed by women as a group. Their behavior seems to qualify as evidence that women need to be tamed or subordinated, reinforcing a fear and suspicion of women and supporting the play's implicit assertion that a proper man and husband will be able to control his wife. The need for taming would seem to be perpetual, and the play would seem to mark the masculine inadequacies of Lucentio and Hortensio, both of whom fail to control their wives in the ways Petruchio controls his. Although Lucentio gets the final word—"'Tis a wonder, by your leave, she will be tamed so" (5.2.199)—the doubt implied by the line reveals him to be a sore loser in contrast with the triumphant Petruchio.

Lucentio, however, also rightly reminds us that Petruchio's manhood is balanced on the razor's edge of Katherina's conformity and that we might doubt his success. Petruchio's masculinity, after all, depends on his mastery of Katherina and his control of her will, even though she has proven herself from the start to be as adept at "rope-tricks" as he (1.2.109). Perhaps she too affects a strategic rhetorical posture, much as Petruchio had done when he whisked her from her wedding, one that consolidates the power available to her within the social realities of Shakespeare's time period. Her final speech may recognize the game she must play to achieve the benefits of marriage—benefits that were considerable for women of her class and social position. We lose sight of that when we focus simply on her subordination to Petruchio. Consequently, the rigid gender settlement the play proposes is only ever provisional: the powerful linguistic resistance to patriarchy dramatized in Katherina's wit and her clever insights into the insecurities of masculine behavior may suggest that Petruchio will succeed only as long as Katherina acts on the words of her final speech. And as we have seen, her capacity for causing gender trouble is large. *The Taming of the Shrew* seems to recognize that gender roles are permeable, that they are constructed in the interplay of people and language and are, therefore, open to negotiation. Indeed, the recognition of this porousness might help explain the play's almost paranoid response to the threat that a woman like Katherina supposedly posed to masculinity.

In this regard, we might briefly consider the Induction. What we often take as the main plot of the comedy turns out to be a play-within-a-play, that famous device through which Shakespeare questioned truth. *The Taming of the Shrew* begins as a tale of a drunken tinker, or pot mender, Christopher Sly, who is tricked into believing he is a great lord. As part of the trick he is shown a play, the story of Katherina and Petruchio. The Induction has little to do with the action of the main plot, but thematically it is very apt: the disorderly Sly seemingly comes to believe that he is someone different from what he had thought, and just as Katherina does, he comes to speak another language: in this case he shifts from prose into the blank verse of his supposed betters. The elaborate joke performed at Sly's expense reminds us of the social tension such potential transformations caused in Shakespeare's England. While officially class may have been seen as absolute, in actual fact the rapid growth of commerce in and around London in the late sixteenth and seventeenth centuries made it inevitable that working men (if not exactly drunken men like Sly) would rise in power and social position. Sly's story then hints at the threat that class boundaries were permeable in much the same way that Katherina and Petruchio's story reveals the threat of permeable gender boundaries. This plot, which for reasons unknown is never completed—Sly simply disappears at the end of Act One, scene one—may serve as the ultimate reminder that the story of Katherina and Petruchio is after all only a play and that the rigid gender roles that come at its end are no more substantial than fiction.

Shakespeare and His England
by David Scott Kastan

S hakespeare is a household name, one of those few that don't need a first name to be instantly recognized. His first name was, of course, William, and he (and it, in its Latin form, *Gulielmus*) first came to public notice on April 26, 1564, when his baptism was recorded in the parish church of Stratford-upon-Avon, a small market town about ninety miles northwest of London. It isn't known exactly when he was born, although traditionally his birthday is taken to be April 23rd. It is a convenient date (perhaps too convenient) because that was the date of his death in 1616, as well as the date of St. George's Day, the annual feast day of England's patron saint. It is possible Shakespeare was born on the 23rd; no doubt he was born within a day or two of that date. In a time of high rates of infant mortality, parents would not wait long after a baby's birth for the baptism. Twenty percent of all children would die before their first birthday.

Life in 1564, not just for infants, was conspicuously vulnerable. If one lived to age fifteen, one was likely to live into one's fifties, but probably no more than 60 percent of those born lived past their mid-teens. Whole towns could be ravaged by epidemic disease. In 1563, the year before Shakespeare was born, an outbreak of plague claimed over one third of the population of London. Fire, too, was a constant threat; the thatched roofs of many houses were highly flammable, as well as offering handy nesting places for insects and rats. Serious crop failures in several years of the decade of the 1560s created food short-ages, severe enough in many cases to lead to the starvation of the elderly and the infirm, and lowering the resistances of many others so that between 1536 and 1560 influenza claimed over 200,000 lives.

Shakespeare's own family in many ways reflected these unsettling realities. He was one of eight children, two of whom did not survive their first year, one of whom died at age eight; one lived to twenty-seven, while the four surviving siblings died at ages ranging from Edmund's thirty-nine to William's own fifty-two years. William married at an unusually early age. He was only eighteen, though his wife was twenty-six, almost exactly the norm of the day for women, though men normally married also in their mid- to late twenties. Shakespeare's wife Anne was already pregnant at the time that the marriage was formally confirmed, and a daughter, Susanna, was born six months later, in May 1583. Two years later, she gave birth to twins, Hamnet and Judith. Hamnet would die in his eleventh year.

If life was always at risk from what Shakespeare would later call "the thousand natural shocks / That flesh is heir to" (*Hamlet*, 3.1.61–62), the incessant threats to peace were no less unnerving, if usually less immediately life threatening. There were almost daily rumors of foreign invasion and civil war as the Protestant Queen Eliz-abeth assumed the crown in 1558 upon the death of her Catholic half sister, Mary. Mary's reign had been marked by the public burnings of Protestant "heretics," by the seeming subordination of England to Spain, and by a commitment to a ruinous war with France, that, among its other effects, fueled inflation and encouraged a debasing of the currency. If, for many, Elizabeth represented the hopes for a peaceful and prosperous Protestant future, it seemed unlikely in the early days of her rule that the young monarch could hold her England together against the twin menace of the powerful Catholic monarchies of Europe and the significant part of her own population who were reluctant to give up their old faith. No wonder the Queen's principal secretary saw England in the early years of Elizabeth's rule as a land surrounded by "perils many, great and imminent."

In Stratford-upon-Avon, it might often have been easy to forget what threatened from without. The simple rural life, shared by about 90 percent of the English populace, had its reassuring natural rhythms and delights. Life was structured by the daily rising and setting of the sun, and by the change of seasons. Crops were planted and harvested; livestock was bred, its young delivered; sheep were sheared, some livestock slaughtered. Market days and fairs saw the produce and crafts of the town arrayed as people came to sell and shop—and be entertained by musicians, dancers, and troupes of actors. But even in Stratford, the lurking tensions and dangers could be daily sensed. A few months before Shakespeare was born, there had been a shocking "defacing" of images in the church, as workmen, not content merely to whitewash over the religious paintings decorating the interior as they were ordered, gouged large holes in those felt to be too "Catholic"; a few months after Shakespeare's birth, the register of the same church records another deadly outbreak of plague. The sleepy market town on the northern bank of the gently flowing river Avon was not immune from the menace of the world that surrounded it.

This was the world into which Shakespeare was born. England at his birth was still poor and backward, a fringe nation on the periphery of Europe. English itself was a minor language, hardly spoken outside of the country's borders. Religious tension was inescapable, as the old Catholic faith was trying determinedly to hold on, even as Protestantism was once again anxiously trying to establish itself as the national religion. The country knew itself vulnerable to serious threats both from without and from within. In 1562, the young Queen, upon whom so many people's hopes rested, almost fell victim to smallpox, and in 1569 a revolt of the Northern earls tried to remove her from power and restore Catholicism as the national religion. The following year, Pope

Pius V pronounced the excommunication of "Elizabeth, the pretended queen of England" and forbade Catholic subjects obedience to the monarch on pain of their own excommunication. "Now we are in an evil way and going to the devil," wrote one clergyman, "and have all nations in our necks."

It was a world of dearth, danger, and domestic unrest. Yet it would soon dramatically change, and Shakespeare's literary contribution would, for future generations, come to be seen as a significant measure of England's remarkable transformation. In the course of Shakespeare's life, England, hitherto an unsophisticated and under-developed backwater acting as a bit player in the momentous political dramas taking place on the European continent, became a confident, prosperous, global presence. But this new world was only accidentally, as it is often known today, "The Age of Shakespeare." To the degree that historical change rests in the hands of any individual, credit must be given to the Queen. This new world arguably was "The Age of Elizabeth," even if it was not the Elizabethan Golden Age, as it has often been portrayed.

The young Queen quickly imposed her personality upon the nation. She had talented councilors around her, all with strong ties to her of friendship or blood, but the direction of government was her own. She was strong willed and cautious, certain of her right to rule and convinced that stability was her greatest responsibility. The result may very well have been, as historians have often charged, that important issues facing England were never dealt with head-on and left to her successors to settle, but it meant also that she was able to keep her England unified and for the most part at peace.

Religion posed her greatest challenge, though it is important to keep in mind that in this period, as an official at Elizabeth's court said, "Religion and the commonwealth cannot be parted asunder." Faith then was not the largely voluntary commitment it is today, nor was there any idea of some separation of church and state. Religion was literally a matter of life and death, of salvation and damnation, and the Church was the Church of England. Obedience to it was not only a matter of conscience but also of law. It was the single issue on which the nation was most likely to be torn apart.

Elizabeth's great achievement was that she was successful in ensuring that the Church of England became formally a Protestant Church, but she did so without either driving most of her Catholic subjects to sedition or alienating the more radical Protestant community. The so-called "Elizabethan Settlement" forged a broad Christian community of what has been called prayer-book Protestantism, even as many of its practitioners retained, as a clergyman said, "still a smack and savor of popish principles." If there were forces on both sides who were uncomfortable with the Settlement—committed Protestants, who wanted to do away with all vestiges of the old faith, and convinced Catholics, who continued to swear their allegiance to Rome—the majority of the country, as she hoped, found ways to live comfortably both within the law and within their faith. In 1571, she wrote to the Duke of Anjou that the forms of worship she recommended would "not properly compel any man to alter his opinion in the great matters now in controversy in the Church." The official toleration of religious ambiguity, as well as the familiar experience of an official change of state religion accompanying the crowning of a new monarch, produced a world where the familiar labels of Protestant and Catholic failed to define the forms of faith that most English people practiced. But for Elizabeth, most matters of faith could be left to individuals, as long as the Church itself, and Elizabeth's position at its head, would remain unchallenged.

In international affairs, she was no less successful with her pragmatism and willingness to pursue limited goals. A complex mix of prudential concerns about religion, the economy, and national security drove her foreign policy. She did not have imperial ambitions; in the main, she wanted only to be sure there would be no invasion of England and to encourage English trade. In the event, both goals brought England into conflict with Spain, determining the increasingly anti-Catholic tendencies of English foreign policy and, almost accidentally, England's emergence as a world power. When Elizabeth came to the throne, England was in many ways a mere satellite nation to the Netherlands, which was part of the Hapsburg Empire that the Catholic Philip II (who had briefly and unhappily been married to her predecessor and half sister, Queen Mary) ruled from Spain; by the end of her reign England was Spain's most bitter rival.

The transformation of Spain from ally to enemy came in a series of small steps (or missteps), no one of which was intended to produce what in the end came to pass. A series of posturings and provocations on both sides led to the rupture. In 1568, things moved to their breaking point, as the English confiscated a large shipment of gold that the Spanish were sending to their troops in the Netherlands. The following year saw the revolt of the Catholic earls in Northern England, followed by the papal excommunication of the Queen in 1570, both of which were by many in England assumed to be at the initiative, or at very least with the tacit support, of Philip. In fact he was not involved, but England under Elizabeth would never again think of Spain as a loyal friend or reliable ally. Indeed, Spain quickly became its mortal enemy. Protestant Dutch rebels had been opposing the Spanish domination of the Netherlands since the early 1560s, but, other than periodic financial support, Elizabeth had done little to encourage them. But in 1585, she sent troops under the command of the Earl of Leicester to support the Dutch rebels against the Spanish. Philip decided then to launch a full-scale attack on England, with the aim of deposing Elizabeth and restoring the Catholic faith. An English assault on Cadiz in 1587 destroyed a number of Spanish ships, postponing Philip's plans, but in the summer of 1588 the mightiest navy in the world, Philip's grand armada, with 132 ships and 30,493 sailors and troops, sailed for England.

By all rights, it should have been a successful invasion, but a combination of questionable Spanish tactics and a fortunate shift of wind resulted in one of England's greatest victories. The English had twice failed to intercept the armada off the coast of Portugal, and the Spanish fleet made its way to England, almost catching the English ships resupplying in Plymouth. The English navy was on its heels, when conveniently the Spanish admiral decided to anchor in the English Channel off the French port of Calais to wait for additional troops coming from the Netherlands. The English attacked with fireships, sinking four Spanish galleons, and strong winds from the south prevented an effective counterattack from the Spanish. The Spanish fleet was pushed into the North Sea, where it regrouped and decided its safest course was to attempt the difficult voyage home around Scotland and Ireland, losing almost half its ships on the way. For many in England the improbable victory was a miracle, evidence of God's favor for Elizabeth and the Protestant nation. Though war with Spain would not end for another fifteen years, the victory over the armada turned England almost overnight into a major world power, buoyed by confidence that they were chosen by God and, more tangibly, by a navy that could compete for control of the seas.

From a backward and insignificant Hapsburg satellite, Elizabeth's England had become, almost by accident, the leader of Protestant Europe. But if the victory over the armada signaled England's new place in the world, it hardly marked the end of England's travails. The economy, which initially was fueled by the military buildup, in the early 1590s fell victim to inflation, heavy taxation to support the war with Spain, the inevitable wartime disruptions of trade, as well as crop failures and a general economic downturn in Europe. Ireland, over which England had been attempting to impose its rule since 1168, continued to be a source of trouble and great expense (in some years costing the crown nearly one fifth of its total revenues). Even when the most organized of the rebellions, begun in 1594 and led by Hugh O'Neill, Earl of Tyrone, formally ended in 1603, peace and stability had not been achieved.

But perhaps the greatest instability came from the uncertainty over the succession, an uncertainty that marked Elizabeth's reign from its beginning. Her near death from smallpox in 1562 reminded the nation that an unmarried queen could not insure the succession, and Elizabeth was under constant pressure to marry and produce an heir. She was always aware of and deeply resented the pressure, announcing as early as 1559: "this shall be for me sufficient that a marble stone shall declare that a queen, having reigned such a time, lived and died a virgin." If, however, it was for her "sufficient," it was not so for her advisors and for much of the nation, who hoped she would wed. Arguably Elizabeth was the wiser, knowing that her unmarried hand was a political advantage, allowing her to diffuse threats or create alliances with the seeming possibility of a match. But as with so much in her reign, the strategy bought temporary stability at the price of longer-term solutions.

By the mid 1590s, it was clear that she would die unmarried and without an heir, and various candidates were positioning themselves to succeed her. Enough anxiety was produced that all published debate about the succession was forbidden by law. There was no direct descendant of the English crown to claim rule, and all the claimants had to reach well back into their family history to find some legitimacy. The best genealogical claim belonged to King James VI of Scotland. His mother, Mary, Queen of Scots, was the granddaughter of James IV of Scotland and Margaret Tudor, sister to Elizabeth's father, Henry VIII. Though James had right on his side, he was, it must be remembered, a foreigner. Scotland shared the island with England but was a separate nation. Great Britain, the union of England and Scotland, would not exist formally until 1707, but with Elizabeth's death early in the morning of March 24, 1603, surprisingly uneventfully the thirty-seven-year-old James succeeded to the English throne. Two nations, one king: King James VI of Scotland, King James I of England.

Most of his English subjects initially greeted the announcement of their new monarch with delight, relieved that the crown had successfully been transferred without any major disruption and reassured that the new King was married with two living sons. However, many quickly became disenchanted with a foreign King who spoke English with a heavy accent, and dismayed even further by the influx of Scots in positions of power. Nonetheless, the new King's greatest political liability may well have been less a matter of nationality than of temperament: he had none of Elizabeth's skill and ease in publicly wooing her subjects. The Venetian ambassador wrote back to the doge that the new King was unwilling to "caress the people, nor make them that good cheer the late Queen did, whereby she won their loves."

He was aloof and largely uninterested in the daily activities of governing, but he was interested in political theory and strongly committed to the cause of peace. Although a steadfast Protestant, he lacked the reflexive anti-Catholicism of many of his subjects. In England, he achieved a broadly consensual community of Protestants. The so-called King James Bible, the famous translation published first in 1611, was the result of a widespread desire to have an English Bible that spoke to all the nation, transcending the religious divisions that had placed three different translations in the hands of his subjects. Internationally, he styled himself *Rex Pacificus* (the peace-loving king). In 1604, the Treaty of London brought Elizabeth's war with Spain formally to an end, and over the next decade he worked to bring about political marriages that might cement stable alliances. In 1613, he married his daughter to the leader of the German Protestants, while the following year he began discussions with Catholic Spain to marry his son to the Infanta Maria. After some ten years of negotiations, James's hopes for what was known as the Spanish match were finally abandoned, much to the delight of the nation, whose long-felt fear and hatred for Spain outweighed the subtle political logic behind the plan.

But if James sought stability and peace, and for the most part succeeded in his aims (at least until 1618, when the bitter religio-political conflicts on the European continent swirled well out of the King's control), he never really achieved concord and cohesion. He ruled over two kingdoms that did not know, like, or even want to understand one another, and his rule did little to bring them closer together. His England remained separate from his Scotland, even as he ruled over both. And even his England remained self divided, as in truth it always was under Elizabeth, ever more a nation of prosperity and influence but still one forged out of deep-rooted divisions of means, faiths, and allegiances that made the very nature of English identity a matter of confusion and concern. Arguably this is the very condition of great drama—sufficient peace and prosperity to support a theater industry and sufficient provocation in the troubling uncertainties about what the nation was and what fundamentally mattered to its people to inspire plays that would offer tentative solutions or at the very least make the troubling questions articulate and moving.

Nine years before James would die in 1625, Shakespeare died, having returned from London to the small market town in which he was born. If London, now a thriving modern metropolis of well over 200,000 people, had, like the nation itself, been transformed in the course of his life, the Warwickshire market town still was much the same. The house in which Shakespeare was born still stood, as did the church in which he was baptized and the school in which he learned to read and write. The river Avon still ran slowly along the town's southern limits. What had changed was that Shakespeare was now its most famous citizen, and, although it would take more than another 100 years to fully achieve this, he would in time become England's, for having turned the great ethical, social, and political issues of his own age into plays that would live forever.

William Shakespeare: A Chronology

1558	**November 17: Queen Elizabeth crowned**
1564	April 26: Shakespeare baptized, third child born to John Shakespeare and Mary Arden
1564	**May 27: Death of Jean Calvin in Geneva**
1565	John Shakespeare elected alderman in Stratford-upon-Avon
1568	**Publication of the Bishops' Bible**
1568	September 4: John Shakespeare elected Bailiff of Stratford-upon-Avon
1569	**Northern Rebellion**
1570	**Queen Elizabeth excommunicated by the pope**
1572	**August 24: St. Bartholomew's Day Massacre in Paris**
1576	**The Theatre built in Shoreditch**
1577–1580	**Sir Francis Drake sails around the world**
1582	November 27: Shakespeare and Anne Hathaway married (Shakespeare is 18)
1583	Queen's Men formed
1583	May 26: Shakespeare's daughter, Susanna, baptized
1584	**Failure of the Virginia Colony**

1585   February 2: Twins, Hamnet and Judith, baptized (Shakespeare is 20)

1586   Babington Plot to dethrone Elizabeth and replace her with Mary, Queen of Scots

1587   February 8: Execution of Mary, Queen of Scots

1587   Rose Theatre built

1588   August: Defeat of the Spanish armada (Shakespeare is 24)

1588   September 4: Death of Robert Dudley, Earl of Leicester

1590   First three books of Spenser's *Faerie Queene* published; Marlowe's *Tamburlaine* published

1592   March 3: *Henry VI, Part One* performed at the Rose Theatre (Shakespeare is 27)

1593   February–November: Theaters closed because of plague

1593   Publication of *Venus and Adonis*

1594   Publication of *Titus Andronicus*, first play by Shakespeare to appear in print (though anonymously)

1594   Lord Chamberlain's Men formed

1595   March 15: Payment made to Shakespeare, Will Kemp, and Richard Burbage for performances at court in December, 1594

1595   Swan Theatre built

1596   Books 4–6 of *The Faerie Queene* published

1596   August 11: Burial of Shakespeare's son, Hamnet (Shakespeare is 32)

1596–1599   Shakespeare living in St. Helen's, Bishopsgate, London

1596   October 20: Grant of Arms to John Shakespeare

1597   May 4: Shakespeare purchases New Place, one of the two largest
        houses in Stratford (Shakespeare is 33)

1598   Publication of *Love's Labor's Lost*, first extant play with Shakespeare's
        name on the title page

1598   Publication of Francis Meres's *Palladis Tamia*, citing Shakespeare as
        "the best for Comedy and Tragedy" among English writers

1599   Opening of the Globe Theatre

**1601   February 7: Lord Chamberlain's Men paid 40 shillings to
        play *Richard II* by supporters of the Earl of Essex, the day
        before his abortive rebellion**

1601   February 17: Execution of Robert Devereaux, Earl of Essex

1601   September 8: Burial of John Shakespeare

1602   May 1: Shakespeare buys 107 acres of farmland in Stratford

**1603   March 24: Queen Elizabeth dies; James VI of Scotland
        succeeds as James I of England** (Shakespeare is 39)

1603   May 19: Lord Chamberlain's Men reformed as the King's Men

1604   Shakespeare living with the Mountjoys, a French Huguenot
        family, in Cripplegate, London

**1604   First edition of Marlowe's *Dr. Faustus* published
        (written c. 1589)**

1604   March 15: Shakespeare named among "players" given scarlet
        cloth to wear at royal procession of King James

1604   Publication of authorized version of *Hamlet* (Shakespeare is 40)

1605   Gunpowder Plot

1605   June 5: Marriage of Susanna Shakespeare to John Hall

1608   Publication of *King Lear* (Shakespeare is 44)

1608–1609   Acquisition of indoor Blackfriars Theatre by King's Men

1609   *Sonnets* published

1611   King James Bible published (Shakespeare is 47)

1612   November 6: Death of Henry, eldest son of King James

1613   February 14: Marriage of King James's daughter Elizabeth to Frederick, the Elector Palatine

1613   March 10: Shakespeare, with some associates, buys gatehouse in Blackfriars, London

1613   June 29: Fire burns the Globe Theatre

1614   Rebuilt Globe reopens

1616   February 10: Marriage of Judith Shakespeare to Thomas Quiney

1616   March 25: Shakespeare's will signed

1616   April 23: Shakespeare dies (age 52)

1616   April 23: Cervantes dies in Madrid

1616   April 25: Shakespeare buried in Holy Trinity Church in Stratford-upon-Avon

1623   August 6: Death of Anne Shakespeare

1623   October: Prince Charles, King James's son, returns from Madrid, having failed to arrange his marriage to Maria Anna, Infanta of Spain

1623   First Folio published with 36 plays (18 never previously published)

Words, Words, Words: Understanding Shakespeare's Language
by David Scott Kastan

I t is silly to pretend that it is easy to read Shakespeare. Reading Shakespeare isn't like picking up a copy of *USA Today* or *The New Yorker*, or even F. Scott Fitzgerald's *Great Gatsby* or Toni Morrison's *Beloved*. It is hard work, because the language is often unfamiliar to us and because it is more concentrated than we are used to. In the theater it is usually a bit easier. Actors can clarify meanings with gestures and actions, allowing us to get the general sense of what is going on, if not every nuance of the language that is spoken. "Action is eloquence," as Volumnia puts it in *Coriolanus*, "and the eyes of th' ignorant / More learnèd than the ears" (3.276–277). Yet the real greatness of Shakespeare rests not on "the general sense" of his plays but on the specificity and suggestiveness of the words in which they are written. It is through language that the plays' full dramatic power is realized, and it is that rich and robust language, often pushed by Shakespeare to the very limits of intelligibility, that we must learn to understand. But we can come to understand it (and enjoy it), and this essay is designed to help.

Even experienced readers and playgoers need help. They often find that his words are difficult to comprehend. Shakespeare sometimes uses words no longer current in English or with meanings that have changed. He regularly multiplies words where seemingly one might do as well or even better. He characteristically writes sentences that are syntactically complicated and imaginatively dense. And it isn't just we, removed by some 400 years from his world, who find him difficult to read; in his own time, his friends and fellow actors knew Shakespeare was hard. As two of them, John Hemings and Henry Condell, put it in their prefatory remarks to Shakespeare's First Folio in 1623, "read him, therefore, and again and again; and if then you do not like him, surely you are in some manifest danger not to understand him."

From the very beginning, then, it was obvious that the plays both deserve and demand not only careful reading but continued re-reading—and that not to read Shakespeare with all the attention a reader can bring to bear on the language is almost to guarantee that a reader will not "understand him" and remain among those who "do not like him." But Shakespeare's colleagues were nonetheless confident that the plays exerted an attraction strong enough to ensure and reward the concentration of their readers, confident, as they say, that in them "you will find enough, both to draw and hold you." The plays do exert a kind of magnetic pull, and have successfully drawn in and held readers for over 400 years.

Once we are drawn in, we confront a world of words that does not always immediately yield its delights; but it will—once we learn to see what is demanded of us. Words in Shakespeare do a lot, arguably more than anyone else has ever asked them to do. In part, it is because he needed his words to do many things at once. His stage had no sets and few props, so his words are all we have to enable us to imagine what his characters see. And they also allow us to see what the characters don't see, especially about themselves. The words are vivid and immediate, as well as complexly layered and psychologically suggestive. The difficulties they pose are not the "thee's" and "thou's" or "prithee's" and "doth's" that obviously mark the chronological distance between Shakespeare and us. When Gertrude says to Hamlet, "thou hast thy father much offended"

(3.4.8), we have no difficulty understanding her chiding, though we might miss that her use of the "thou" form of the pronoun expresses an intimacy that Hamlet pointedly refuses with his reply: "Mother, *you* have my father much offended" (3.4.9; italics mine).

Most deceptive are words that look the same as words we know but now mean something different. Words often change meanings over time. When Horatio and the soldiers try to stop Hamlet as he chases after the Ghost, Hamlet pushes past them and says, "I'll make a ghost of him that lets me" (1.4.85). It seems an odd thing to say. Why should he threaten someone who "lets" him do what he wants to do? But here "let" means "hinder," not, as it does today, "allow" (although the older meaning of the word still survives, for example, in tennis, where a "let serve" is one that is hindered by the net on its way across). There are many words that can, like this, mislead us: "his" sometimes means "its," "an" often means "if," "envy" means something more like "malice," "cousin" means more generally "kinsman," and there are others, though all are easily defined. The difficulty is that we may not stop to look thinking we already know what the word means, but in this edition a ° following the word alerts a reader that there is a gloss in the left margin, and quickly readers get used to these older meanings.

Then, of course, there is the intimidation factor—strange, polysyllabic, or Latinate words that not only are foreign to us but also must have sounded strange even to Shakespeare's audiences. When Macbeth wonders whether all the water in all the oceans of the world will be able to clean his bloody hands after the murder of Duncan, he concludes: "No; this my hand will rather / The multitudinous seas incarnadine, / Making the green one red" (2.2.64–66). Duncan's blood staining Macbeth's murderous hand is so offensive that, not merely does it resist being washed off in water, but it will "the multitudinous seas incarnadine": that is, turn the sea-green oceans blood-red. Notes will easily clarify the meaning of the two odd words, but it is worth observing that they would have been as odd to Shakespeare's readers as they are to us. The *Oxford English Dictionary (OED)* shows no use of "multitudinous" before this, and it records no use of "incarnadine" before 1591 (*Macbeth* was written about 1606). Both are new words, coined from the Latin, part of a process in Shakespeare's time where English adopted many Latinate words as a mark of its own emergence as an important vernacular language. Here they are used to express the magnitude of Macbeth's offense, a crime not only against the civil law but also against the cosmic order, and then the simple monosyllables of turning "the green one red" provide an immediate (and needed) paraphrase and register his own sickening awareness of the true hideousness of his deed.

As with "multitudinous" in *Macbeth*, Shakespeare is the source of a great many words in English. Sometimes he coined them himself, or, if he didn't invent them, he was the first person whose writing of them has survived. Some of these words have become part of our language, so common that it is hard to imagine they were not always part of it: for example, "assassination" (*Macbeth*, 1.7.2), "bedroom" (*A Midsummer Night's Dream*, 2.2.57), "countless" (*Titus Andronicus*, 5.3.59), "fashionable" (*Troilus and Cressida*, 3.3.165), "frugal" (*The Merry Wives of Windsor*, 2.1.28), "laughable" (*The Merchant of Venice*, 1.1.56), "lonely" (*Coriolanus*, 4.1.30), and "useful" (*King John*, 5.2.81). But other words that he originated were not as, to use yet another Shakespearean coinage, "successful" (*Titus Andronicus*, 1.1.66). Words like "crimeless" (*Henry VI, Part Two*, 2.4.63, meaning "innocent"), "facinorous" (*All's Well That Ends Well*, 2.3.30, meaning "extremely wicked"), and "recountment" (*As You Like It*, 4.3.141, meaning "narrative" or "account") have, without much resistance, slipped into oblivion. Clearly Shakespeare liked words, even unwieldy ones. His working vocabulary, about 18,000 words, is staggering, larger than almost any other English writer, and he seems to be the first person to use in print about 1,000 of these. Whether he coined the new words himself or was intrigued by the new words he heard in the streets of London doesn't really matter; the point is that he was remarkably alert to and engaged with a dynamic language that was expanding in response to England's own expanding contact with the world around it.

But it is neither new words nor old ones that are the source of the greatest difficulty of Shakespeare's language. The real difficulty (and the real delight) comes in trying to see how he uses the words, how he endows them with more than their denotative meanings. Why, for example, does Macbeth say that he hopes that the "sure and firm-set earth" (2.1.56) will not hear his steps as he goes forward to murder Duncan? Here "sure" and "firm-set" mean virtually the same thing: stable, secure, fixed. Why use two words? If this were a student paper, no doubt the teacher would circle one of them and write "redundant." But the redundancy is exactly what Shakespeare wants. One word would do if the purpose were to describe the solidity of the earth, but here the redundancy points to something different. It reveals something about Macbeth's mind, betraying through the doubling how deep is his awareness of the world of stable values that the terrible act he is about to commit must unsettle.

Shakespeare's words usually work this way: in part describing what the characters see and as often betraying what they feel. The example from *Macbeth* is a simple example of how this works. Shakespeare's words are carefully patterned. How one says something is every bit as important as what is said, and the conspicuous patterns that are created alert us to the fact that something more than the words' lexical sense has been put into play. Words can be coupled, as in the example above, or knit into even denser metaphorical constellations to reveal something about the speaker (which often the speaker does not know), as in Prince Hal's promise to his father that he will outdo the rebels' hero, Henry Percy (Hotspur):

Percy is but my factor, good my lord,

To engross up glorious deeds on my behalf,

And I will call him to so strict account

That he shall render every glory up,

Yea, even the slightest worship of his time,

Or I will tear the reckoning from his heart.

                                    (Henry IV, Part One, 3.2.147–152)

The Prince expresses his confidence that he will defeat Hotspur, but revealingly in a reiterated language of commercial exchange ("factor," "engross," "account," "render," "reckoning") that tells us something important both about the Prince and the ways in which he understands his world. In a play filled with references to coins and counterfeiting, the speech demonstrates not only that Hal has committed himself to the business at hand, repudiating his earlier, irresponsible tavern self, but also that he knows it is a business rather than a glorious world of chivalric achievement; he inhabits a world in which value (political as well as economic) is not intrinsic but determined by what people are willing to invest, and he proves himself a master of producing desire for what he has to offer.

Or sometimes it is not the network of imagery but the very syntax that speaks, as when Claudius announces his marriage to Hamlet's mother:

Therefore our sometime sister, now our Queen,

Th' imperial jointress to this warlike state,

Have we—as 'twere with a defeated joy,

With an auspicious and a dropping eye,

With mirth in funeral and with dole in marriage,

In equal scale weighing delight and dole—

Taken to wife.   *(Hamlet, 1.2.8–14)*

All he really wants to say here is that he has married Gertrude, his former sister-in-law: "Therefore our sometime sister . . . Have we . . . Taken to wife." But the straightforward sentence gets interrupted and complicated, revealing his own discomfort with the announcement. His elaborations and intensifications of Gertrude's role ("sometime sister," "Queen," "imperial jointress"), the self-conscious rhetorical balancing of the middle three lines (indeed "in equal scale weighing delight and dole"), all declare by the all-too obvious artifice how desperate he is to hide the awkward facts behind a veneer of normalcy and propriety. The very unnaturalness of the sentence is what alerts us that we are meant to understand more than the simple relation of fact.

Why doesn't Shakespeare just say what he means? Well, he does—exactly what he means. In the example from *Hamlet* just above, Shakespeare shows us something about Claudius that Claudius doesn't know himself. Always Shakespeare's words will offer us an immediate sense of what is happening, allowing us to follow the action, but they also offer us a counterplot, pointing us to what might be behind the action, confirming or contradicting what the characters say. It is a language that shimmers with promise and possibility, opening the characters' hearts and minds to our view—and all we have to do is learn to pay attention to what is there before us.

Shakespeare's Verse

Another distinctive feature of Shakespeare's dramatic language is that much of it is in verse. Almost all of the plays mix poetry and prose, but the poetry dominates. *The Merry Wives of Windsor* has the lowest percentage (only about 13 percent verse), while *Richard II* and *King John* are written entirely in verse (the only examples, although *Henry VI, Part One* and *Part Three* have only a very few prose lines). In most of the plays, about 70 percent of the lines are written in verse.

Shakespeare's characteristic verse line is a non-rhyming iambic pentameter ("blank verse"), ten syllables with every second one stressed. In *A Midsummer Night's Dream*, Titania comes to her senses after a magic potion has led her to fall in love with an ass-headed Bottom: "Methought I was enamored of an ass" (4.1.76). Similarly, in *Romeo and Juliet*, Romeo gazes up at Juliet's window: "But soft, what light through yonder window breaks" (2.2.2). In both these examples, the line has ten syllables organized into five regular beats (each beat consisting of the stress on the second syllable of a pair, as in "But soft," the da-dum rhythm forming an "iamb"). Still, we don't hear these lines as jingles; they seem natural enough, in large part because this dominant pattern is varied in the surrounding lines.

The play of stresses indeed becomes another key to meaning, as Shakespeare alerts us to what is important. In *Measure for Measure*, Lucio urges Isabella to plead for her brother's life: "Oh, to him, to him, wench! He will relent" (2.2.129). The iambic norm (unstressed-stressed) tells us (and an actor) that the emphasis at the beginning of the line is on "to" not "him"—it is the action not the object that is being emphasized—and at the end of the line the stress falls on "will." Alternatively, the line can play against the established norm. In *Hamlet*, Claudius corrects Polonius's idea of what is bothering the Prince: "Love? His affections do not that way tend" (3.1.161). The iambic norm forces the emphasis onto "that" ("do not *that* way tend"), while the syntax forces an unexpected stress on the opening word, "Love." In the famous line, "The course of true love never did run smooth" (*A Midsummer Night's Dream*, 1.1.134), the iambic expectation is varied in both the middle and at the end of the line. Both "love" and the first syllable of "never" are stressed, as are both syllables at the end—"run smooth"— which creates a metrical foot in which both syllables are stressed (called a "spondee"). The point to notice is that the "da-dum, da-dum, da-dum, da-dum, da-dum" line is not inevitable; it merely sets an expectation against which many variations can be heard.

In fact, even the ten-syllable norm can be varied. Shakespeare sometimes writes lines with fewer or more syllables. Often there is an extra, unstressed syllable at the end of a line (a so-called "feminine ending"); sometimes there are verse lines with only nine. In *Henry IV, Part One*, King Henry replies incredulously to the rebel Worcester's claim that he hadn't "sought" the confrontation with the King: "You have not sought it? How comes it then?" (5.1.27). There are only nine syllables here (some earlier editors, seeking to "correct" the verse, added the word "sir" after the first question to regularize the line). But the pause where one expects a stressed syllable is dramatically effective, allowing the King's anger to be powerfully present in the silence.

As even these few examples show, Shakespeare's verse is unusually flexible, allowing a range of rhythmical effects. It should not be understood as a set of strict rules but as a flexible set of practices rooted in dramatic necessity. It is designed to highlight ideas and emotions, and it is based less upon rigid syllable counts than on an arrangement of stresses within an understood temporal norm, as one might expect from a poetry written to be heard in the theater rather than read on the page.

Here Follows Prose

Although the plays are dominated by verse, prose plays a significant role. Shakespeare's prose has its own rhythms, but it lacks the formal patterning of verse, and so is printed without line breaks and without the capitals that mark the beginning of a verse line. Like many of his fellow dramatists, Shakespeare tended to use prose for comic scenes, the shift from verse serving, especially in his early plays, as a social marker. Upper-class characters speak in verse; lower-class characters speak in prose. Thus, in *A Midsummer Night's Dream*, the Athenians of the court, as well as the fairies, all speak in verse, but the "rude mechanicals," Bottom and his artisan friends, all speak in prose, except for the comic verse they speak in their performance of "Pyramis and Thisbe."

As Shakespeare grew in experience, he became more flexible about the shifts from verse to prose, letting it, among other things, mark genre rather than class and measure various kinds of intensity. Prose becomes in the main the medium of comedy. The great comedies, like *Much Ado About Nothing*, *Twelfth Night*, and *As You Like It*, are all more than 50 percent prose. But even in comedy, shifts between verse and prose may be used to measure subtle emotional changes. In Act One, scene three of *The Merchant of Venice*, Shylock and Bassanio begin the scene speaking of matters of business in prose, but when Antonio enters and the deep conflict between the Christian and the Jew becomes evident, the scene shifts to verse. But prose may itself serve in moments of emotional intensity. Shylock's famous speech in Act Three, scene one, "Hath not a Jew eyes . . ." is all in prose, as is Hamlet's expression of disgust at the world ("I have of late— but wherefore I know not—lost all my mirth . . .") at 3.1.51–64. Shakespeare comes to use prose to vary the tone of a scene, as the shift from verse subtly alerts an audience or a reader to some new emotional register.

Prose becomes, as Shakespeare's art matures, not inevitably the mark of the lower classes but the mark of a salutary daily-ness. It is appropriately the medium in which letters are written, and it is the medium of a common sense that will at least challenge the potential self-deceptions of grandiloquent speech. When Rosalind mocks the excesses and artifice of Orlando's wooing in Act Four, scene one of *As You Like It*, it is in prose that she seeks something genuine in the expression of love:

> The poor world is almost six thousand years old, and in all this time there was not any man died in his own person, *videlicit* [i.e., namely], in a love cause. . . . Men have died from time to time, and worms have eaten them, but not for love.

Here the prose becomes the sound of common sense, an effective foil to the affectation of pinning poems to trees and thinking that it is real love.

It is not that prose is artless; Shakespeare's prose is no less self-conscious than his verse. The artfulness of his prose is different, of course. The seeming ordinariness of his prose is no less an effect of his artistry than is the more obvious patterning of his verse. Prose is no less serious, compressed, or indeed figurative. As with his verse, Shakespeare's prose performs numerous tasks and displays various, subtle formal qualities; and recognizing the possibilities of what it can achieve is still another way of seeing what Shakespeare puts right before us to show us what he has hidden.

Further Reading

N. F. Blake, *Shakespeare's Language: An Introduction* (New York: St. Martin's Press, 1983).

Jonathan Hope, *Shakespeare's Grammar* (London: Thomson, 2003).

Sister Miriam Joseph, *Shakespeare's Use of the Arts of Language* (New York:Columbia University Press, 1947).

M. M. Mahood, *Shakespeare's Wordplay* (London: Methuen, 1957).

Russ McDonald, *Shakespeare and the Arts of Language* (Oxford: Oxford University Press, 2001).

Brian Vickers, *The Artistry of Shakespeare's Prose* (London: Methuen, 1968).

George T. Wright, *Shakespeare's Metrical Art* (Berkeley: Univ. of California Press, 1991).

Key to the Play Text

Symbols

°   Indicates an explanation or definition in the left-hand margin.

1   Indicates a gloss on the page facing the play text.

[ ]   Indicates something added or changed by the editors (i.e., not in the early printed text that this edition of the play is based on).

Terms

F, *Folio*, or *First Folio* — The first collected edition of Shakespeare's plays, published in 1623, and the basis for this edition (see Editing *The Taming of the Shrew*, page 299).

The Taming of
the Shrew

William Shakespeare

List of Roles

1   Induction

The first two scenes of the play form an *Induction*, a term first used for this material by Alexander Pope in 1723. Such introductory scenes were common in the drama of the 1580s and 1590s, and they often called attention to the staged or fictional nature of the play to follow, thus inviting the audience to speculate on the nature of truth or reality as it was being represented. See LONGER NOTE on page 293.

2   *in faith*

A mild oath, similar to "By God"

3   *A pair of stocks*

I.e., "I'll put you in the stocks." Used to punish petty criminals, the stocks consisted of a bench placed behind a wooden board with holes, into which the offender's legs (and sometimes wrists) would be locked. Unable to move, the criminal was then publicly displayed in the town square.

4   *chronicles*

History books

5   *Richard Conqueror*

Sly confuses the names of two early English kings, "Richard the Lionhearted" and "William the Conqueror."

6   paucas pallabris

I.e., *pocas palabras* ("few words" in Spanish). The phrase was known in part because of its use in Thomas Kyd's popular play *The Spanish Tragedy.*

7   Sessa!

The precise meaning of this word is unclear; Sly may mean *cesa* (Spanish for "be quiet"), *cessez* (French for "cease"), or *sasa* (a German expression meaning "run quickly," which here would mean "go away").

8   *denier*

A French copper coin worth less than a cent

9   *Go by, Saint Jeronimy.*

Sly misquotes another popular line from *The Spanish Tragedy*, in which the hero is warned "Hieronimo, beware! Go by; go by!" Sly has conflated the name of the play's hero, Hieronimo, with that of Saint Jerome. *Go by* is a dismissive phrase, like "forget it."

10   *by law*

According to the law; in court

11   *boy*

Used as a general term of contempt

12   *Breathe Merriman*

Let Merriman (one of the hounds) rest

13   *deep-mouthed brach*

Low-voiced bitch. Hounds that could howl in a very low register were especially prized by hunters.

14   *made it good*

Found the scent

Induction,[1] Scene 1

*Enter [**Sly**] and the* **Hostess**.

Sly

get even with   I'll feeze °you, in faith.[2]

Hostess

A pair of stocks,[3] you rogue!

Sly

slut   You're a baggage;° the Slys are no rogues. Look in the
chronicles[4]—we came in with Richard Conqueror.[5]

go by   Therefore, *paucas pallabris,*[6] let the world slide.° *Sessa!*[7]   5

Hostess

You will not pay for the glasses you have burst?

Sly

No, not a denier.[8] Go by, Saint Jeronimy.[9] Go to thy
cold bed and warm thee.

Hostess

constable   I know my remedy. I must go fetch the thirdborough.°

[She exits.]

Sly

Third, or fourth, or fifthborough, I'll answer him by law.[10]   10

welcome   I'll not budge an inch, boy.[11] Let him come, and kindly.°

[He] falls asleep.

Blow   *Wind° horns.*

attendants   *Enter a* **Lord** *from hunting, with his train.*°

Lord

order / treat   Huntsman, I charge° thee, tender° well my hounds.

exhausted   Breathe Merriman[12]— the poor cur is embossed °—

leash together   And couple ° Clowder with the deep-mouthed brach.[13]

Saw'st thou not, boy, how Silver made it good[14]   15

45

1   *in the coldest fault*

> I.e., when the scent was almost lost
> (a break in the scent being followed
> was called a *fault*)

2   *pound*

> I.e., pounds. (The *pound* was the
> basic monetary unit of 16th-
> century England, comprised of 20
> shillings or 240 pence.)

3   *merest loss*

> I.e., when the scent was almost
> completely gone

4   *image*

> Likeness (the sleeping Sly is the
> *image* of *death*.)

5   *banquet*

> A selection of fruits and other
> snacks (not a full meal)

6   *forget himself*

> Lose his sense of his own identity

7   *he cannot choose*

> He'd have to

At the hedge corner, in the coldest fault?[1]
I would not lose the dog for twenty pound.[2]
First Huntsman
Why, Belman is as good as he, my lord.
howled He cried° upon it at the merest loss[3]
And twice today picked out the dullest scent.   20
Trust me: I take him for the better dog.
Lord
fast Thou art a fool. If Echo were as fleet, °
I would esteem him worth a dozen such.
feed / after But sup° them well and look unto° them all.
Tomorrow I intend to hunt again.   25
First Huntsman
I will, my lord.
Lord
What's here? One dead or drunk? See doth he
      breathe.
Second Huntsman
He breathes, my lord. Were he not warmed with ale,
too This were a bed but° cold to sleep so soundly.
Lord
O monstrous beast! How like a swine he lies!   30
Grim death, how foul and loathsome is thine image![4]
play a trick Sirs, I will practice° on this drunken man.
What think you? If he were conveyed to bed,
perfumed Wrapped in sweet° clothes, rings put upon his fingers,
A most delicious banquet[5] by his bed,   35
well-dressed And brave° attendants near him when he wakes,
Would not the beggar then forget himself?[6]
First Huntsman
Believe me, lord, I think he cannot choose.[7]
Second Huntsman
incredible It would seem strange° unto him when he waked.

1   *wanton pictures*

   Erotic paintings

2   *he is*

   I.e., who he is

3   *kindly*

   Naturally (i.e., convincingly)

4   *husbanded with modesty*

   **Performed with moderation; not
   overdone (see line 91 and note)**

Lord

fantasy   Even as a flatt'ring dream or worthless fancy.°   *40*

    Then take him up and manage well the jest.

    Carry him gently to my fairest chamber

    And hang it round with all my wanton pictures. ¹

Bathe/purified   Balm° his foul head in warm distillèd° waters

sweetsmelling   And burn sweet° wood to make the lodging sweet.   *45*

    Procure me music ready when he wakes

melodious   To make a dulcet° and a heavenly sound.

immediately   And if he chance to speak, be ready straight°

curtsy; bow   And, with a low submissive reverence,°

    Say, "What is it your Honor will command?"   *50*

    Let one attend him with a silver basin

    Full of rose-water and bestrewed with flowers,

pitcher/towel   Another bear the ewer,° the third a diaper,°

    And say, "Will 't please your Lordship cool your

        hands?"

    Someone be ready with a costly suit   *55*

    And ask him what apparel he will wear.

    Another tell him of his hounds and horse

    And that his lady mourns at his disease.

insane   Persuade him that he hath been lunatic,°

    And when he says he is,² say that he dreams,   *60*

    For he is nothing but a mighty lord.

    This do, and do it kindly,³ gentle sirs.

surpassingly   It will be pastime passing° excellent

    If it be husbanded with modesty.⁴

First Huntsman

guarantee   My lord, I warrant° you we will play our part   *65*

So that   As° he shall think, by our true diligence,

    He is no less than what we say he is.

Lord

    Take him up gently and to bed with him,

1   *Sirrah*

    A common form of address to
    servants or other inferiors (pro-
    nounced with emphasis on the first
    syllable)

2   *repose him*

    Rest himself

3   *players*

    Actors. Professional acting compa-
    nies often toured in Shakespeare's
    time, most often when the London
    theaters were closed because of
    plague.

4   *aptly fitted*

    Suitable to your talents

5   *Soto*

    The reference has not been cer-
    tainly identified. A character called
    Soto appears in John Fletcher's
    play *Women Pleased*, but as it seems
    to have been written about 1620,
    much later than *The Taming of the
    Shrew*, most scholars believe that
    Shakespeare is referring to a char-
    acter in an earlier play, now lost,
    which Fletcher may have revised.
    The speech itself is assigned in the
    Folio to "Sincklo"; John Sincklo was
    an actor in Shakespeare's company,
    and seemingly Shakespeare here
    wrote in the name of the actor he
    had in mind for the role instead of
    the character's name.

assignment And each one to his office° when he wakes.

             [*Some servants carry out Sly.*] *Sound trumpets.*

      Sirrah,[1] go see what trumpet 'tis that sounds.   70

                    [*A servingman exits.*]

Perhaps Belike° some noble gentleman that means,

      Traveling some journey, to repose him[2] here.

          Enter **Servingman.**

      How now! Who is it?

      Servingman

If   An° 't please your Honor, players[3]

      That offer service to your Lordship.

          Enter **Players.**

      Lord

      Bid them come near.   75

      Now, fellows, you are welcome.

      Players

      We thank your Honor.

      Lord

      Do you intend to stay with me tonight?

      A Player

If it / service So° please your Lordship to accept our duty.°

      Lord

      With all my heart. This fellow I remember   80

      Since once he played a farmer's eldest son.

      —'Twas where you wooed the gentlewoman so well.

      I have forgot your name, but sure that part

      Was aptly fitted[4] and naturally performed.

      A Player

      I think 'twas Soto[5] that your Honor means.   85

1 *in happy time*
At the perfect time

2 *The rather for*
I.e., particularly since

3 *heard*
In Elizabethan England, a play was often referred to as something one heard rather than saw (hence "audience")

4 *veriest antic*
Most complete buffoon

5 *page*
A young man attending on a lord

6 *him dressed in all suits like a lady*
In Shakespeare's time all female parts were played by adolescent boys; the first English actresses appeared on the professional stage only after 1660.

7 *Do him obeisance.*
Do him reverence; treat him with respect.

8 *as he will*
If he wishes to

9 *He bear himself with honorable action*
I.e., he should behave in a dignified manner.

10 *soft low tongue*
Gentle voice

11 *lowly courtesy*
Humble curtsies

Lord

excellently 'Tis very true. Thou didst it excellent.°

Well, you are come to me in happy time,¹

The rather for² I have some sport in hand

skill Wherein your cunning° can assist me much.

There is a lord will hear you play tonight;   90

self-restraint But I am doubtful of your modesties,°

In case / while observing Lest° over-eyeing° of his odd behavior

(For yet his Honor never heard³ a play)

laughing fit You break into some merry passion°

And so offend him. For I tell you, sirs,   95

If you should smile, he grows impatient.

A Player

Fear not, my lord, we can contain ourselves

Were he the veriest antic⁴ in the world.

Lord

pantry [*to a servingman*] Go, sirrah; take them to the buttery°

And give them friendly welcome every one.   100

lack / provides Let them want° nothing that my house affords.°

[*A servingman*] *exits with the* **Players**.

Sirrah, go you to Barthol'mew, my page,⁵

aspects And see him dressed in all suits° like a lady.⁶

That done, conduct him to the drunkard's chamber

And call him "madam." Do him obeisance.⁷   105

Tell him from me, as he will⁸ win my love,

He bear himself with honorable action,⁹

Such as he hath observed in noble ladies

performed Unto their lords, by them accomplishèd.°

Such duty to the drunkard let him do   110

With soft low tongue¹⁰ and lowly courtesy,¹¹

And say, "What is 't your Honor will command,

Wherein your lady and your humble wife

May show her duty and make known her love?"

1   *And with declining head into his bosom*

The lord could mean either that the
Page should hang his head as a sign
of deep concern or that he should
rest his head on Sly's chest.

2   *commanded tears*

Tears on cue

3   *close conveyed*

Secretly carried

4   *in despite*

I.e., despite the fact that the Page is
unable to cry on cue

5   *in to counsel*

Go in to instruct

6   *May well abate the over-merry spleen*

May well calm the bursts of laughter. (Bursts of laughter and other
powerful emotions were believed
to be generated by the *spleen*.)

7   *grow into extremes*

Get out of hand

embraces	And then with kind embracements,° tempting kisses, 115
	And with declining head into his bosom, ¹
	Bid him shed tears, as being overjoyed
	To see her noble lord restored to health,
himself	Who for this seven years hath esteemed him°
	No better than a poor and loathsome beggar. 120
	And if the boy have not a woman's gift
	To rain a shower of commanded tears, ²
purpose	An onion will do well for such a shift,°
	Which in a napkin being close conveyed³
	Shall in despite⁴ enforce a watery eye. 125
	See this dispatched with all the haste thou canst.
Soon	Anon° I'll give thee more instructions.

A servingman exits.

assume	I know the boy will well usurp° the grace,
walk	Voice, gait,° and action of a gentlewoman.
	I long to hear him call the drunkard "husband," 130
keep	And how my men will stay° themselves from laughter
	When they do homage to this simple peasant.
Perhaps	I'll in to counsel⁵ them. Haply° my presence
	May well abate the over-merry spleen⁶
	Which otherwise would grow into extremes. ⁷ 135

[They exit.]

1   aloft

Possibly this means that Sly and the attendants enter on the balcony (see Fig. 1 on page 306), though, given the number of actors and the necessary bed, a temporary platform could have been built above the main stage, which would offer more space and bring the action forward.

2   appurtenances

Accessories

3   *sack*

A type of Spanish white wine; *sack* was expensive and therefore more appropriate than *small ale* for a gentleman.

4   *conserves of beef*

Salted beef

5   *my toes look through the over-leather*

Show my toes through (holes in) the top of the shoe

6   *idle humor*

Foolish behavior

7   *Burton Heath*

Probably Burton-on-the-Heath, a village not far from Stratford-upon-Avon, where Shakespeare grew up and where his family continued to live. As does the reference to *Wincot* in line 21, the reference to a

recognizable English place-name may help create a degree of distance between Shakespeare's audience and the somewhat troubling tale about wife taming in the main plot, which is clearly set in Italy.

8   *cardmaker*

One who manufactures *cards*, metal combs used to prepare wool for spinning

9   *bearherd*

A keeper of a performing bear

10   *tinker*

A mender of pots or metalworker. Tinkers were proverbially quarrelsome and foul mouthed.

11   *alewife*

A woman who runs a tavern. The name *Marian Hacket* possibly refers to a real person, though it is unclear whether this *alewife* is the same woman as the *Hostess* who appears in the opening scene.

12   *Wincot*

A small village a few miles south of Stratford-upon-Avon

Induction, Scene 2

Enter aloft [1] [**Sly**] *the drunkard, with* [**Servingmen**], *some with apparel, others with basin and ewer and other appurtenances,* [2] *and* **Lord**.

Sly

weak   For God's sake, a pot of small° ale.

First Servingman

Will 't please your Lordship drink a cup of sack? [3]

Second Servingman

candied fruit   Will 't please your Honor taste of these conserves? °

Third Servingman

clothing   What raiment° will your Honor wear today?

Sly

I am Christophero Sly. Call not me "Honor" nor "Lord-   5
ship." I ne'er drank sack in my life, and if you give me
any conserves, give me conserves of beef. [4] Ne'er ask me
clothing/jackets   what raiment° I'll wear, for I have no more doublets°
than backs, no more stockings than legs, nor no more
sometimes   shoes than feet, nay sometime° more feet than shoes,   10
or such shoes as my toes look through the over-
leather. [5]

Lord

Heaven cease this idle humor [6] in your Honor!
ancestry   Oh, that a mighty man of such descent, °
Of such possessions and so high esteem,   15
infected   Should be infusèd° with so foul a spirit!

Sly

What, would you make me mad? Am not I Christopher
Sly, old Sly's son of Burton Heath, [7] by birth a peddler, by
change   education a cardmaker, [8] by transmutation° a bearherd, [9]
and now by present profession a tinker? [10] Ask Marian   20
Hacket, the fat alewife [11] of Wincot, [12] if she know me not!

1   *on the score*

In debt. Tavern accounts were recorded by *scoring* or cutting notches
on a stick, wall, or door.

2   *sheer ale*

I.e., ale alone (without food)

3   *score me up for*

Mark me up as; consider me

4   *Hence comes it that*

This is why

5   *bethink thee of*

Remember

6   *trimmed up*

Prepared

7   *Semiramis*

A queen of ancient Assyria, notorious for her sexual exploits

8   *bestrow the ground*

Cover the ground (with rushes or
flowers)

9   *hawking*

Hunting for small game with
trained hawks, a popular aristocratic sport

10   *fetch shrill echoes from the hollow Earth*

I.e., cause the Earth to echo shrilly

11   *breathèd*

Of great stamina

12   *roe*

A small deer known for its speed

13   *Dost thou love pictures?*

The subject matter of the paintings
described in lines 49–59 derives
from Ovid's *Metamorphoses*, a classical Latin poem, whose stories
about the miraculous transformations of various characters
drawn from mythology exerted a
profound influence on Shakespeare throughout his career. The
topics suggest these may be quasi-
pornographic paintings, perhaps
the *wanton pictures* mentioned in
scene 1, line 43. They reveal the
decadence of the upper-class lord
in contrast to the more homespun
Sly. They also, perhaps, comment
on the inherent eroticism of watching as Sly and the audience prepare
to watch a play about another transformation, i.e., Katherina's.

14   *Adonis*

In Greek legend, a youth whose
physical beauty enchanted the
goddess Venus as she watched him
bathe (see Ovid's *Metamorphoses*, X,
and Shakespeare's narrative poem
Venus and Adonis, published in 1593)

If she say I am not fourteen pence on the score[1]
for sheer ale,[2] score me up for[3] the lying'st knave in
i.e., crazy Christendom. What! I am not bestraught!° Here's—
Third Servingman
Oh, this it is that makes your lady mourn!   25
Second Servingman
Oh, this is it that makes your servants droop!
Lord
family Hence comes it that[4] your kindred° shuns your house,
As if they were As° beaten hence by your strange lunacy.
O noble lord, bethink thee of[5] thy birth,
former Call home thy ancient° thoughts from banishment   30
And banish hence these abject lowly dreams.
Look how thy servants do attend on thee,
duty / summons Each in his office° ready at thy beck.°
Greek god of music Wilt thou have music? Hark! Apollo° plays,   *Music*
And twenty cagèd nightingales do sing.   35
Or wilt thou sleep? We'll have thee to a couch
Softer and sweeter than the lustful bed
On purpose trimmed up[6] for Semiramis.[7]
Say thou wilt walk, we will bestrow the ground.[8]
adorned Or wilt thou ride? Thy horses shall be trapped,°   40
Their harness studded all with gold and pearl.
that will Dost thou love hawking?[9] Thou hast hawks will° soar
Above the morning lark. Or wilt thou hunt?
sky Thy hounds shall make the welkin° answer them
And fetch shrill echoes from the hollow Earth.[10]   45
First Servingman
hunt with hounds Say thou wilt course.° Thy greyhounds are as swift
swifter As breathèd[11] stags, ay, fleeter° than the roe.[12]
Second Servingman
Dost thou love pictures?[13] We will fetch thee straight
Adonis[14] painted by a running brook

1   *Cytherea*

Another name for Venus, goddess of love, who was born off the coast of *Cythera* (which is the root of the name)

2   *Io*

A virgin raped by the god Jupiter, who surprised her by hiding himself in a cloud; she was later transformed into a cow to hide her from his wife, Juno (see Ovid's *Metamorphoses*, I).

3   *As lively painted as the deed was done*

Painted so realistically, it seems as lifelike as the deed itself.

4   *Daphne*

A nymph who infatuated the god Apollo; he tried to rape her but she was saved by the river god Peneus, who changed her into a laurel tree (see Ovid's *Metamorphoses*, I).

5   *in this waning age*

In this degenerate time. In the Elizabethan view of human history, it was commonly believed that the world had once existed in a state of grace or perfection (epitomized by the biblical Garden of Eden or the classical Golden Age) but was since then steadily deteriorating.

6   *Am I a lord, and have I such a lady?*

As Sly begins to believe that he might be a lord, he begins to speak in verse.

7   *our*

Now fully convinced of his status, Sly adopts the "royal plural," a form of self-reference used by monarchs to indicate their authority.

<table>
<tr><td>reeds; marsh grass</td><td>And Cytherea¹ all in sedges° hid,</td><td>50</td></tr>
<tr><td>dance seductively</td><td>Which seem to move and wanton° with her breath,</td><td></td></tr>
<tr><td></td><td>Even as the waving sedges play with wind.</td><td></td></tr>
</table>

Lord

We'll show thee Io² as she was a maid,

deceived   And how she was beguilèd° and surprised,

As lively painted as the deed was done.³   55

Third Servingman

Or Daphne⁴ roaming through a thorny wood,

so that   Scratching her legs that° one shall swear she bleeds,

And at that sight shall sad Apollo weep,

skillfully   So workmanly° the blood and tears are drawn.

Lord

Thou art a lord and nothing but a lord.   60

Thou hast a lady far more beautiful

Than any woman in this waning age.⁵

First Servingman

And till the tears that she hath shed for thee

malicious / overran   Like envious° floods o'errun° her lovely face,

She was the fairest creature in the world—   65

still   And yet° she is inferior to none.

Sly

Am I a lord, and have I such a lady?⁶

Or do I dream? Or have I dreamed till now?

I do not sleep: I see, I hear, I speak.

aromas   I smell sweet savors° and I feel soft things.   70

Upon my life, I am a lord indeed

And not a tinker, nor Christopher Sly.

Well, bring our lady hither to our⁷ sight,

weakest   And, once again, a pot o' the smallest° ale.

[A servingman exits.]

Second Servingman

Will 't please your Mightiness to wash your hands?   75

1   *knew but*

    Only knew

2   *beaten out of door*

    Thrown outside

3   *present her at the leet*

    Bring her before the manorial court. On large estates or manors, the lord of the manor could preside over his own court and issue rulings and punishments.

4   *Because she brought stone jugs and no sealed quarts*

    I.e., because she shortchanged her customers. *Sealed quarts* **were quart jugs marked with a seal guaranteeing their size; a plain, unmarked stone jug could appear to hold a quart yet, in reality, contain less.**

5   *the woman's maid of the house*

    The hostess's maid. *Cecily* **could be related to Marian Hacket (see lines 20–21) or perhaps is an error for that name.**

6   *reckoned up*

    Mentioned

7   *Greece*

    Possibly *Greet,* **an English village not far from Stratford-upon-Avon; the names mentioned in lines 92–93 may represent real people known to Shakespeare, but this has not been proven.**

8   *Thou shalt not lose by it.*

    I.e., you'll be rewarded for it (your care of me).

sanity; intellect   Oh, how we joy to see your wit° restored!

Oh, that once more you knew but¹ what you are!

These fifteen years you have been in a dream,

Or, when you waked, so waked as if you slept.

Sly

i.e., faith   These fifteen years? By my fay, ° a goodly nap.   80

in   But did I never speak of° all that time?

First Servingman

foolish   O, yes, my lord, but very idle° words,

For though you lay here in this goodly chamber,

Yet would you say ye were beaten out of door, ²

tavern   And rail upon the hostess of the house, °   85

And say you would present her at the leet³

Because she brought stone jugs and no sealed quarts. ⁴

Sometimes you would call out for Cicely Hacket.

Sly

Ay, the woman's maid of the house. ⁵

Third Servingman

Why, sir, you know no house nor no such maid,   90

Nor no such men as you have reckoned up, ⁶

As Stephen Sly and old John Naps of Greece, ⁷

And Peter Turph and Henry Pimpernell,

And twenty more such names and men as these,

Which never were, nor no man ever saw.   95

Sly

recovery   Now Lord be thankèd for my good amends!°

All

Amen.

Sly

I thank thee. Thou shalt not lose by it. ⁸

*Enter [the **Page** as a] Lady, with attendants.*

1   *Marry*

A shortened form of "By the Virgin
Mary," regularly used as a mild oath
meaning something like "indeed"

2   *I fare well*

Both "I am well" and "I have good
fare" (i.e., food and drink)

3   *Being all this time abandoned from your*
bed

The convention of the boy actor
playing female roles was usually
taken for granted, as seems to be
the case here. In an effort to sound
convincing as Sly's make-believe
wife, the Page feigns an intense
feeling of sexual abandonment during the many years "her" so-called
husband has supposedly been ill.
Taking the Page's words at face
value, Sly comically decides that he
has been remiss in his duty as a husband and orders "her" to undress
and come immediately to bed. In
this case, the audience knows that
the Page is a boy or young man, so
Sly's eagerness becomes, clearly, a
joke at the tinker's expense. But the
scene does suggest that boy actors
could play convincingly desirable
women. Sly's taking the Page for
a woman is no different from any
member of Shakespeare's audience
accepting Katherina or Bianca, also
played by boys, as women.

Page

How fares my noble lord?

Sly

                                        Marry, [1] I fare well, [2]

food and drink   For here is cheer° enough. Where is my wife?   100

Page

Here, noble lord. What is thy will with her?

Sly

Are you my wife and will not call me "husband"?

husband   My men should call me "lord." I am your goodman.°

Page

My husband and my lord, my lord and husband,

I am your wife in all obedience.   105

Sly

I know it well.—What must I call her?

Lord

                                        "Madam."

Sly

"Alice Madam," or "Joan Madam"?

Lord

"Madam" and nothing else. So lords call ladies.

Sly

Madam wife, they say that I have dreamed

over   And slept above° some fifteen year or more.   110

Page

Ay, and the time seems thirty unto me,

banished   Being all this time abandoned° from your bed. [3]

Sly

a long time   'Tis much. °—Servants, leave me and her alone.

                                [**Lord** *and* **Servingmen** *exit.*]

yourself   Madam, undress you° and come now to bed.

Page

Thrice noble lord, let me entreat of you   115

To pardon me yet for a night or two,

1   *expressly charged*

Specifically ordered

2   *In peril to incur your former malady*

At the risk of causing a relapse of your former illness

3   *yet absent me*

Still keep myself away

4   *stands for*

Serves as

5   *it stands so that I may hardly tarry so long*

A lewd pun; i.e., my penis *stands so* (is so erect) that I don't think I can wait that long.

6   *would be loath*

Would hate

7   *tarry in despite of the flesh and the blood*

Wait in spite of my sexual desire

8   *hearing your amendment*

Hearing of your recovery

9   *congealed your blood*

Elizabethan doctors believed that *sadness* or *melancholy* could cause the blood to thicken, which in turn could cause fits of insanity, or *frenzy*.

10   *frame your mind to*

Focus your attention on

11   *a Christmas gambold or a tumbling-trick*

I.e., a Christmas entertainment (*gambold* is Sly's mispronunciation of "gambol") or an acrobatic trick

Or, if not so, until the sun be set.
For your physicians have expressly charged, [1]
In peril to incur your former malady, [2]
That I should yet absent me [3] from your bed.   120
I hope this reason stands for [4] my excuse.

Sly

Ay, it stands so that I may hardly tarry so long. [5] But I

delusions would be loath [6] to fall into my dreams° again. I will
therefore tarry in despite of the flesh and the blood. [7]

Enter a **Messenger**.

Messenger

Your Honor's players, hearing your amendment, [8]   125
Are come to play a pleasant comedy,

appropriate For so your doctors hold it very meet, °
Seeing too much sadness hath congealed your blood, [9]
And melancholy is the nurse of frenzy.
Therefore they thought it good you hear a play   130
And frame your mind to [10] mirth and merriment,

prevents Which bars° a thousand harms and lengthens life.

Sly

i.e., comedy Marry, I will. Let them play it. Is not a comonty° a
Christmas gambold or a tumbling-trick? [11]

Page

No, my good lord, it is more pleasing stuff.   135

Sly

furnishings What, household stuff? °

Page

story   It is a kind of history.°

Sly

Well, we'll see 't. Come, madam wife, sit by my side and

pass by let the world slip.° We shall ne'er be younger.

[*They sit.*]

1 man
   Servant

2 **Tranio**
   See **LONGER NOTE**, page 294.

3 *since for*
   Because of

4 *Padua, nursery of arts*
   Padua had a world-renowned uni-
   versity, which was founded in 1228.

5 *fruitful Lombardy*
   Lombardy is used imprecisely to re-
   fer to the north of Italy, which was
   the main agricultural area of Italy.
   (Padua is actually in the Veneto.)

6 *well approved in all*
   Very reliable in everything

7 *ingenious studies*
   I.e., liberal studies (studies appro-
   priate for a nobleman)

8 *my father first*
   My father before me

9 *come of*
   Descended from

10 *It shall become to serve all hopes*
   conceived / To deck his fortune with his
   virtuous deeds
   It will fulfill the expectations
   my family has for me if my life
   combines my father's wealth with
   his virtue.

11 *treats of happiness / By virtue specially to*
   be achieved
   Considers how happiness can be
   achieved through virtuous behavior
   (i.e., the argument of Aristotle's
   ***Ethics*)**

12 Mi perdonato
   Pardon me (Italian)

13 *I am in all affected as yourself*
   I feel about everything exactly as
   you do.

Act 1, Scene 1

Flourish. Enter **Lucentio** *and his man* [1] **Tranio.** [2]

Lucentio

Tranio, since for [3] the great desire I had

To see fair Padua, nursery of arts, [4]

at   I am arrived for° fruitful Lombardy, [5]

The pleasant garden of great Italy,

permission / equipped   And, by my father's love and leave, ° am armed°   5

With his good will and thy good company.

My trusty servant, well approved in all, [6]

rest / perhaps   Here let us breathe° and haply° institute

A course of learning and ingenious studies. [7]

learned   Pisa, renownèd for grave° citizens,   10

Gave me my being and my father first, [8]

business   A merchant of great traffic° through the world,

Vincentio, come of [9] the Bentivolii.

i.e., Lucentio   Vincentio's son, ° brought up in Florence,

It shall become to serve all hopes conceived   15

To deck his fortune with his virtuous deeds. [10]

i.e., time being   And therefore, Tranio, for the time° I study

Virtue, and that part of philosophy

Will I apply that treats of happiness

By virtue specially to be achieved. [11]   20

Tell me thy mind, for I have Pisa left

And am to Padua come, as he that leaves

pool / himself   A shallow plash° to plunge him° in the deep

excess   And with satiety° seeks to quench his thirst.

Tranio

Mi perdonato, [12] gentle master mine.   25

I am in all affected as yourself, [13]

Glad that you thus continue your resolve

To suck the sweets of sweet philosophy.

1   *Let's be no stoics nor no stocks*

The *Stoics* were a Greek school of
philosophers who believed in the
restraint of emotions and the rejec-
tion of worldly comforts; *stocks*
were wooden posts (and therefore
incapable of feeling).

2   *Or so devote to Aristotle's checks / As Ovid*
be an outcast quite abjured

Or be so committed to Aristotle's
moral rigor that Ovid is completely
rejected. Aristotle was a Greek phi-
losopher (see p. 68, note 11); Ovid
was the Roman poet well known for
erotic poetry such as *Metamorphoses*
and *The Art of Love*.

3   *Balk logic with acquaintance that you*
have

Reject scholastic logic in favor of
knowledge you already have.

4   *rhetoric*

The art of public speaking

5   *Fall to them as you find your stomach*
serves you

Engage in them as your appetite for
them dictates.

6   *Gramercies*

Many thanks (derived from the Old
French phrase *grant merci*)

7   *If, Biondello, thou wert come ashore*

Lucentio addresses his absent
servant, Biondello, as if he
were present. (The reference to
ashore is either an error, in which
Shakespeare imagines Padua as a
seaport, or a reference to the river
system that indeed connects a
number of northern Italian cities.)

8   *put us in readiness*

Make ourselves ready

9   a pantaloon

In the Italian *commedia dell'arte*, the
pantaloon was a comic figure representing traditional authority in
the guise of a foolish old man, and
in subsequent English theatrical
tradition he was often a frustrated
rival for the love of the young heroine. Traditionally a pantaloon wore
a skullcap, Turkish slippers, and
close-fitting red tights, emphasizing his decayed legs and suggesting his physical inadequacy as a
suitor for the heroine. There is no
direct evidence that Gremio would
have been dressed this way on
Shakespeare's stage, but it seems
possible given the play's emphasis
on his inadequacy (sexual and otherwise) as a suitor to Bianca.

Only, good master, while we do admire
This virtue and this moral discipline,   30
Let's be no stoics nor no stocks,[1] I pray,
Or so devote to Aristotle's checks
As Ovid be an outcast quite abjured.[2]
Balk logic with acquaintance that you have,[3]
everyday   And practice rhetoric[4] in your common° talk;   35
poetry / enliven   Music and poesy° use to quicken° you;
The mathematics and the metaphysics,
Fall to them as you find your stomach serves you.[5]
i.e., taken   No profit grows where is no pleasure ta'en.°
enjoy   In brief, sir, study what you most affect.°   40
Lucentio
Gramercies,[6] Tranio, well dost thou advise.
If, Biondello, thou wert come ashore,[7]
We could at once put us in readiness[8]
And take a lodging fit to entertain
create; provide   Such friends as time in Padua shall beget.°   45

Enter **Baptista** *with his two daughters,* **Katherina**
and **Bianca**, **Gremio**, *a pantaloon,*[9] *[and]* **Hortensio**, *suitor to* **Bianca**.

But stay awhile. What company is this?
Tranio
Master, some show to welcome us to town.
                          Lucentio *[and]* **Tranio** *stand by.*
Baptista
plead with   Gentlemen, importune° me no farther,
For how I firmly am resolved you know—
That is, not to bestow my youngest daughter   50
Before I have a husband for the elder.
If either of you both love Katherina,
Because I know you well and love you well,

1   *To cart her*

Baptista has just given Hortensio and Gremio permission to woo Katherina, and Gremio responds by punning on the word *court*. Prostitutes were often placed in carts and driven through town as part of their punishment. Unruly women, or *shrews*, were also sometimes carted and driven through town fitted with painful "scolds' bridles"—metal headpieces with an iron bit that extended into the woman's mouth to depress her tongue and gag her.

2   *make a stale of me amongst these mates*

Make me a laughingstock among these fellows. *Stale* also was a slang term for prostitute, so the first words Katherina speaks pun on Gremio's insult about "carting" her. She verbally resists Baptista's treatment of her and Bianca as objects to be disposed of by him. Her wit appears also in the use of the dismissive term *mates* to describe the two suitors (by which she means "contemptible fellows" but which Hortensio understands as "husbands") and also punning on the word "stalemate," implying that she knows that she is seen as an obstacle to her father's and Bianca's happiness. Kate's extraordinary linguistic facility perhaps marks her as a shrew in the public sphere, where women were largely enjoined to silence, but it also helps characterizes her keen intelligence and vigorous spirit.

3   *it is not halfway to her heart*

It is not even halfway attractive to her (speaking of herself in the third person).

4   *doubt not*

Do not doubt that

5   *comb your noddle*

Beat your head

6   *wench*

Slang for "woman"

7   *wonderful froward*

Incredibly headstrong

Leave shall you have to court her at your pleasure.

Gremio

violent To cart her,[1] rather. She's too rough° for me.   55

There, there, Hortensio, will you any wife?

Katherina

[*to* **Baptista**] I pray you, sir, is it your will

To make a stale of me amongst these mates?[2]

Hortensio

"Mates," maid? How mean you that? No mates for you

character Unless you were of gentler, milder mold.°   60

Katherina

I' faith, sir, you shall never need to fear.

Certainly Iwis° it is not halfway to her heart,[3]

But if it were, doubt not[4] her care should be

To comb your noddle[5] with a three-legged stool

i.e., paint with blood And paint° your face and use you like a fool.   65

Hortensio

From all such devils, good Lord, deliver us!

Gremio

And me too, good Lord!

Tranio

i.e., Hush [*aside to* **Lucentio**] Husht,° master, here's some good

about to happen   pastime toward.°

That wench[6] is stark mad or wonderful froward.[7]

Lucentio

[*aside to* **Tranio**] But in the other's silence do I see   70

seriousness; modesty Maid's mild behavior and sobriety.°

Peace, Tranio.

Tranio

Be quiet [*aside to* **Lucentio**] Well said, master. Mum,° and gaze

    your fill.

1   *peat*

    Young woman (often used, as here, to describe a spoiled girl)

2   *It is best / Put finger in the eye, an she knew why.*

    It would be even better to fake some tears (by putting a *finger in the eye*) if she could think of a good excuse for them.

3   *content you in my discontent*

    Be satisfied with my unhappiness.

4   *Minerva*

    Roman goddess of wisdom and creator of musical instruments

5   *mew her up*

    Keep her caged up

6   *bear the penance of her tongue*

    Be punished for Katherina's bad manners

7   *content ye*

    Be content; that's the way it is.

Baptista
[*to* **Gremio** *and* **Hortensio**] Gentlemen, that I may
    soon make good
What I have said—Bianca, get you in,   75
And let it not displease thee, good Bianca,
For I will love thee ne'er the less, my girl.

Katherina
A pretty peat![1] It is best
if   Put finger in the eye, an° she knew why.[2]

Bianca
Sister, content you in my discontent.[3]   80
will / submit   [*to* **Baptista**] Sir, to your pleasure° humbly I subscribe.°
My books and instruments shall be my company,
On them to look and practice by myself.

Lucentio
Hark, Tranio! Thou may'st hear Minerva[4] speak.

Hortensio
distant; unfriendly   Signior Baptista, will you be so strange?°   85
causes   Sorry am I that our good will effects°
Bianca's grief.

Gremio
                 Why will you mew her up,[5]
because of   Signior Baptista, for° this fiend of Hell,
i.e., Bianca / i.e., Katherina's   And make her° bear the penance of her° tongue?[6]

Baptista
Gentlemen, content ye.[7] I am resolved.   90
Go in, Bianca.   [**Bianca** *exits.*]
because   And for° I know she taketh most delight
In music, instruments, and poetry,
Schoolmasters will I keep within my house
Fit to instruct her youth. If you, Hortensio,   95
Or, Signior Gremio, you know any such,

1 *Prefer them hither*
Recommend them to me.

2 *appointed hours*
Put on a schedule

3 *I knew not what to take and what to leave*
I.e., I was too stupid to be able to make my own decisions.

4 *the devil's dam*
The devil's mother (cf. *Comedy of Errors* 4.3.45–47)

5 *Your gifts are so good here's none will hold you.*
You have such good qualities that none of us will stop you from leaving (with the additional sarcastic sense that Katharine is too good to be anyone's wife).

6 *There! Love is not so great*
Gremio uses "There" as an exclamation also at line 56, but it is possible the line should be "Their love is not so great," meaning that a woman's love is not so important.

7 *we may blow our nails together and fast it fairly out*
We may wait together patiently and refrain from quarreling.

8 *Our cake's dough on both sides.*
I.e., both of us have failed.

9 *light on*
Find

10 *that wherein she delights*
The things she enjoys

11 *brooked parle*
Allowed for negotiaton

12 *labor and effect*
Work to bring about

learned; skillful   Prefer them hither,[1] for to cunning ° men
generous   I will be very kind, and liberal °
                     To mine own children in good bringing up.
                     And so farewell. Katherina, you may stay,   100
discuss   For I have more to commune ° with Bianca.   *He exits.*

Katherina
                     Why, and I trust I may go too, may I not? What, shall I
perhaps   be appointed hours[2] as though, belike, ° I knew not
                     what to take and what to leave?[3] Ha!   *She exits.*

Gremio
                     You may go to the devil's dam![4] Your gifts are so good   105
                     here's none will hold you.[5] There! Love is not so great,[6]
                     Hortensio, but we may blow our nails together and fast
                     it fairly out.[7] Our cake's dough on both sides.[8] Farewell.
                     Yet for the love I bear my sweet Bianca, if I can by any
                     means light on[9] a fit man to teach her that wherein   110
recommend   she delights,[10] I will wish ° him to her father.

Hortensio
                     So will I, Signior Gremio. But a word, I pray. Though
                     the nature of our quarrel yet never brooked parle,[11]
reflection / concerns know now, upon advice, ° it toucheth ° us both, that
                     we may yet again have access to our fair mistress and   115
                     be happy rivals in Bianca's love, to labor and effect[12]
                     one thing specially.

Gremio
                     What's that, I pray?

Hortensio
                     Marry, sir, to get a husband for her sister.

Gremio
                     A husband? A devil!   120

Hortensio
                     I say a husband.

Gremio
                     I say a devil. Think'st thou, Hortensio, though her

1   *Tush*

A common exclamation, equivalent to "Listen" or "For Heaven's sake"

2   *alarums*

I.e., tirades. An *alarum* was a military signal that served as the call to arms, usually a trumpet blast.

3   *light on*

Find

4   *the high cross*

A cross, raised on a platform, marking the town center, where criminals were whipped

5   *bar in law*

Legal restriction (Baptista's decision to *bar* access to Bianca)

6   *it shall be so far forth friendly maintained*

We will continue to maintain our friendship.

7   *have to 't afresh*

We can start fighting once more (over Bianca).

8   *Happy man be his dole!*

I.e., may the best man win.

9   *He that runs fastest gets the ring.*

Proverbial equivalent to "winner takes all." Shakespeare is imagining a jousting contest with riders on horseback competing to thread their lance through a metal ring, but puns also on *ring* as "wedding ring" and also as a euphemism for vagina.

10 *How say you*

What do you say?

much   father be very rich, any man is so very° a fool to be
married to Hell?

Hortensio

exceeds   Tush,¹ Gremio. Though it pass° your patience and mine   125
to endure her loud alarums,² why, man, there be good

if   fellows in the world, an° a man could light on³ them,
would take her with all faults, and money enough.

Gremio

gladly   I cannot tell. But I had as lief° take her dowry with
this condition: to be whipped at the high cross⁴ every   130
morning.

Hortensio

little/between   Faith, as you say, there's small° choice in° rotten apples.
But come, since this bar in law⁵ makes us friends, it
shall be so far forth friendly maintained⁶ till by helping Baptista's eldest daughter to a husband we set his   135
youngest free for a husband, and then have to 't afresh.⁷
Sweet Bianca! Happy man be his dole!⁸ He that runs
fastest gets the ring.⁹ How say you,¹⁰ Signior Gremio?

Gremio

wish   I am agreed, and would° I had given him the best
horse in Padua to begin his wooing that would   140
thoroughly woo her, wed her, and bed her, and rid the
house of her! Come on.

[**Gremio** *and* **Hortensio**] *exit.*
Tranio *and* **Lucentio** *remain.*

Tranio

I pray, sir, tell me, is it possible
That love should of a sudden take such hold?

Lucentio

O Tranio, till I found it to be true,   145
I never thought it possible or likely.

1 *I found the effect of love-in-idleness*

I.e., I fell in love. *Love-in-idleness* was another name for the pansy, a flower whose juice was believed to make people fall in love (as it does in *A Midsummer Night's Dream*, 2.1.170–172).

2 *That art to me as secret and as dear*

Who is to me as intimate and as precious

3 *As Anna to the Queen of Carthage was*

In Virgil's *Aeneid* (circa 29–19 B.C.), Dido is the *Queen of Carthage*, who kills herself after being abandoned by Aeneas, the legendary founder of Rome. *Anna* is Dido's sister, who counseled her to have an affair with Aeneas and who subsequently was the primary mourner at her funeral. Because there were many familiar instances of male friendship in the classical tradition that Lucentio could have invoked, Shakespeare may be implying that his passion for Bianca will lead to his undoing.

4 *I burn, I pine, I perish*

Lucentio uses a courtly Petrarchan language of suffering for love that was for the most part seen as an appropriately masculine form of expression in the period; nevertheless, in *Romeo and Juliet* (circa 1594) Shakespeare explores Romeo's similar use of Petrarchan formulas to describe his love for Rosalind as evidence of emotional immaturity. Lucentio's Petrarchan language may therefore signify a shallow and perhaps emasculating capitulation to female charm. It certainly seems to contrast him with Petruchio, whose wooing of Katherina is anything but courtly and whose aggressive masculinity is expressed in less conventional language.

5 *is not rated from*

Cannot be scolded out of

6 *naught remains but so*

Nothing can be done but this.

7 Redime te captum quam queas minimo

I.e., ransom yourself out of captivity as cheaply as possible (Latin).

8 *so longly*

For so long (though possibly "so longingly")

9 *the pith of all*

The central point

10 *the daughter of Agenor*

I.e., Europa, whom Jove (in Ovid's *Metamorphoses*, II) abducted by transforming himself into a bull and, when she climbed upon his back, carrying her off

11 *humble him to her hand*

Humble himself before her

12 *When with his knees he kissed the Cretan strand*

When he knelt on the shore of Crete

But see, while idly I stood looking on,

I found the effect of love-in-idleness[1]

honesty   And now in plainness° do confess to thee

(That art to me as secret and as dear[2]   150

As Anna to the Queen of Carthage was)[3]

Tranio, I burn, I pine, I perish,[4] Tranio,

win   If I achieve° not this young modest girl.

Advise   Counsel° me, Tranio, for I know thou canst.

Assist me, Tranio, for I know thou wilt.   155

Tranio

scold   Master, it is no time to chide° you now.

Affection is not rated from[5] the heart.

If love have touched you, naught remains but so:[6]

Rédime te captum quam queas minimo.[7]

Lucentio

satisfies me   Gramercies, lad, go forward. This contents.°   160

sensible   The rest will comfort, for thy counsel's sound. °

Tranio

Master, you looked so longly[8] on the maid,

noticed   Perhaps you marked° not what's the pith of all.[9]

Lucentio

Oh, yes, I saw sweet beauty in her face

Such as the daughter of Agenor[10] had,   165

That made great Jove to humble him to her hand[11]

When with his knees he kissed the Cretan strand.[12]

Tranio

Saw you no more? Marked you not how her sister

Began to scold and raise up such a storm

That mortal ears might hardly endure the din?   170

Lucentio

Tranio, I saw her coral lips to move

And with her breath she did perfume the air.

Sacred and sweet was all I saw in her.

1   *curst and shrewd*

    Ill-tempered and sharp-tongued

2   *closely mewed her up*

    Strictly confined her to his house

3   *for my hand*

    I.e., my guess is

4   *Both our inventions meet and jump in one*

    Our thoughts exactly coincide

5   *Keep house and ply his book*

    **Maintain a residence and apply
    himself to his studies**

Tranio

[*aside*] Nay, then, 'tis time to stir him from his trance.

[*to* **Lucentio**] I pray, awake, sir! If you love the maid,   175

Apply; Direct Bend° thoughts and wits to achieve her. Thus it stands:

Her elder sister is so curst and shrewd [1]

That, till the father rid his hands of her,

Master, your love must live a maid at home,

And therefore has he closely mewed her up, [2]   180

So that/ troubled Because° she will not be annoyed° with suitors.

Lucentio

Ah, Tranio, what a cruel father's he!

aware But art thou not advised° he took some care

To get her cunning schoolmasters to instruct her?

Tranio

planned out Ay, marry, am I, sir, and now 'tis plotted!°   185

Lucentio

(i.e., a plan) I have it,° Tranio!

Tranio

Master, for my hand [3]

Both our inventions meet and jump in one. [4]

Lucentio

Tell me thine first.

Tranio

You will be schoolmaster

And undertake the teaching of the maid:

plan That's your device.°

Lucentio

It is. May it be done?   190

Tranio

play Not possible. For who shall bear° your part

And be in Padua here Vincentio's son,

Keep house and ply his book, [5] welcome his friends,

Visit his countrymen and banquet them?

1 *have it full*

Have it all worked out

2 *Uncase thee*

Take off your outer clothing.

3 *colored hat and cloak*

Bright stylish clothing denoted a gentleman. Servants generally wore plainer clothes, often blue or another dark color.

4 *charm*

Persuade, with the additional sense of "cast a spell on"

5 *So had you need.*

I.e., you will have to

6 *I think 'twas in another sense*

I.e., I don't think he meant it quite like this.

7 *Whose sudden sight hath thralled*

Whose sudden appearance has captivated

8 *my wounded eye*

I.e., *wounded* by Cupid's arrow

9 *how now*

A common interjection, meaning "what's this?"

Lucentio

Basta!° Content thee, for I have it full. [1]   195
We have not yet been seen in any house,
Nor can we be distinguished by our faces
For man or master. Then it follows thus:
Thou shalt be master, Tranio, in my stead,
Keep house and port° and servants as I should.   200
I will some other be, some Florentine,
Some Neapolitan, or meaner° man of Pisa.
'Tis hatched and shall be so. Tranio, at once
Uncase thee. [2] Take my colored hat and cloak. [3]

[_They change garments._]

When Biondello comes, he waits on thee,   205
But I will charm [4] him first to keep his tongue.

Tranio

So had you need. [5]
In brief, sir, sith° it your pleasure is,
And I am tied° to be obedient—
For so your father charged° me at our parting: 210
"Be serviceable to my son," quoth he,
Although I think 'twas in another sense. [6]—
I am content to be Lucentio,
Because so well I love Lucentio.

Lucentio

Tranio, be so, because Lucentio loves,   215
And let me be a slave t' achieve that maid
Whose sudden sight hath thralled [7] my wounded eye. [8]

Enter **Biondello**.

Here comes the rogue.°—Sirrah, where have you been?

Biondello

Where have I been? Nay, how now, [9] where are you?

Left margin glosses:

Enough (Italian) (line 195)
position; lifestyle (line 200)
poorer (line 202)
since (line 208)
obligated (line 209)
commanded (line 210)
knave (line 1218)

1   *Pray*

Short for "I pray you" (i.e., please)

2   *frame your manners to the time*

Make your actions appropriate to this situation.

3   *for my escape*

To make my escape

4   *make way from hence*

Get away from here

5   *Ne'er a whit.*

Not even slightly

6   *the next wish after*

The following wish

7   *use your manners discreetly in all kinds of companies*

Behave properly toward everyone we meet

8   *rests that thyself execute: to make one among these wooers*

Remains for you to do: become one of these suitors

9   Presenters

I.e., actors, referring to the actors playing Sly, the Page, and a Servingman left from the Induction

Master, has my fellow Tranio stolen your clothes? Or   220
you stolen his? Or both? Pray, [1] what's the news?
Lucentio

here   Sirrah, come hither. ° 'Tis no time to jest,
And therefore frame your manners to the time. [2]
Your fellow Tranio here, to save my life,

bearing; demeanor   Puts my apparel and my count'nance ° on,   225
And I for my escape [3] have put on his;
For in a quarrel since I came ashore

seen   I killed a man and fear I was descried. °

is suitable   Wait you on him, I charge you, as becomes, °
While I make way from hence [4] to save my life.   230
You understand me?
Biondello
                              Aye, sir. [*aside*] Ne'er a whit. [5]
Lucentio

bit   And not a jot ° of "Tranio" in your mouth.
Tranio is changed into Lucentio.
Biondello

I wish   The better for him. Would ° I were so too.
Tranio

in faith   So would I, faith, ° boy, to have the next wish after: [6]   235
That Lucentio indeed had Baptista's youngest daughter.
But, sirrah, not for my sake, but your master's, I advise
You use your manners discreetly in all kind of companies. [7]
When I am alone, why then I am Tranio,
But in all places else, your master Lucentio.   240
Lucentio
Tranio, let's go. One thing more rests that thyself ex-
ecute: to make one among these wooers. [8] If thou ask

suffice it to say   me why, sufficeth ° my reasons are both good and

important   weighty. °   *They exit.*
                              The Presenters [9] above speak.

1   *by Saint Anne*

     **A mild oath (Saint Anne was,
     according to tradition, the mother
     of the Virgin Mary)**

2   *Would 'twere done.*

     I.e., I wish it were over.

First Servingman

doze / pay attention to   My lord, you nod.° You do not mind° the play.   245

Sly

subject   Yes, by Saint Anne,[1] do I. A good matter,° surely.

Comes there any more of it?

Page

My lord, 'tis but begun.

Sly

'Tis a very excellent piece of work, madam lady. Would

observe   'twere done.[2]   *They sit and mark.°*   250

1   *of all*

Especially

2   *Villain*

The word *villain* originally referred
to any peasant or lower-class
person; in Shakespeare's day it was
frequently used as a general term
of insult rather than in the modern
sense of "criminal."

3   *knock me*

I.e., knock for me. In the next line
Grumio takes *knock me* to mean that
Petruchio himself asks to be struck.

4   *I should knock you first, / And then I know
after who comes by the worst.*

I.e., first I'll hit you, but then I
know I'll get an even worse beating
afterward.

5   *ring it*

Knock at it (*ring* referring to the
round door knocker, but playing
also on "wring" as in the stage
direction)

6   *sol, fa*

I.e., sing the notes of a scale.

7   *masters*

Gentlemen (perhaps comically
directed at the audience or merely a
call for help). The Folio prints "mistris," probably from the compositor
misunderstanding the manuscript
abbreviation "mrs."

Act 1, Scene 2

servant *Enter* **Petruchio** *and his man*° **Grumio.**

Petruchio
Verona, for a while I take my leave
To see my friends in Padua, but of all[1]
My best belovèd and approvèd friend,
think Hortensio. And I trow° this is his house.
Here, sirrah Grumio. Knock, I say.   5
Grumio
Knock, sir? Whom should I knock? Is there any man
i.e., "abused" has rebused° your Worship?
Petruchio
Villain,[2] I say, knock me[3] here soundly.
Grumio
who Knock you here, sir? Why sir, what° am I, sir, that I
should knock you here, sir?   10
Petruchio
Villain, I say, knock me at this gate
head And rap me well, or I'll knock your knave's pate.°
Grumio
My master is grown quarrelsome. I should knock you
     first,
And then I know after who comes by the worst.[4]
Petruchio
Will it not be?   15
if Faith, sirrah, an° you'll not knock, I'll ring it.[5]
test I'll try° how you can sol, fa,[6] and sing it.
                              He wrings him by the ears.
Grumio
Help, masters,[7] help! My master is mad!
Petruchio
Now knock when I bid you, sirrah villain.

1   *part the fray*
    Break up the fight

2   Con tutto il cuore, ben trovato
    With all my heart, well met (Italian)

3   Alla nostra casa ben venuto, molto
    honorato Signior mio Petruchio.
    **Welcome to our house, my most
    honored Signior Petruchio (Italian).**

4   *in Latin*
    **Either Shakespeare has moment-
    arily forgotten that Grumio is
    Italian, or the servant pretends he
    thinks Petruchio's and Hortensio's
    Italian is Latin as part of his deliber-
    ate misunderstanding of his master
    in the first forty lines of the scene.**

5   *for aught I see*
    For all I know

6   *two-and-thirty, a pip out*
    **I.e., drunk and slightly insane. Ap-
    parently *one-and-thirty* was slang for
    "drunk," but the phrase refers to a
    card game called "one-and-thirty,"
    in which the object was to collect
    cards that had a total of thirty-one
    spots (*pips*) on them. Exceeding the
    total meant losing the game; hence
    being *two-and-thirty* made you *a
    pip out*, and in turn *a pip out* became
    slang for "a little insane."**

7   *for my heart*
    For the life of me

Enter **Hortensio**.

Hortensio

How now, what's the matter? My old friend Grumio   20
and my good friend Petruchio? How do you all at
Verona?

Petruchio

Signior Hortensio, come you to part the fray?[1]
Con tutto il cuore, ben trovato,[2] may I say.

Hortensio

Alla nostra casa ben venuto, molto honorato Signior mio Petruchio.[3]   25

settle   Rise, Grumio, rise. We will compound° this quarrel.

Grumio

i.e., alleges   Nay, 'tis no matter, sir, what he 'leges° in Latin.[4] If this
be not a lawful cause for me to leave his service—look
you, sir: he bid me knock him and rap him soundly, sir.
Well, was it fit for a servant to use his master so, being   30
perhaps, for aught I see,[5] two-and-thirty, a pip out?[6]
Whom, would to God, I had well knocked at first,
Then had not Grumio come by the worst.

Petruchio

brainless   A senseless° villain. Good Hortensio,
I bade the rascal knock upon your gate   35
And could not get him, for my heart,[7] to do it.

Grumio

Knock at the gate? O heavens! Spake you not these
words plain: "Sirrah, knock me here, rap me here,
knock me well, and knock me soundly"? And come
you now with "knocking at the gate"?   40

Petruchio

Sirrah, begone or talk not, I advise you.

1 *this' a heavy chance*

This is an unfortunate misunderstanding

2 *happy gale*

Fortunate wind

3 *come roundly to*

Speak plainly with

4 *burden*

The *burden* of a tune was its bass underscore; Petruchio says that *wealth* is the motive underlying his pursuits.

5 *Be she as foul as was Florentius' love, / As old as Sibyl, and as curst and shrewd / As Socrates' Xanthippe*

The women Petruchio mentions are all famously ugly, old, or shrewish. Sir Florent was the knight in John Gower's *Confessio Amantis*, who, to get the answer to a question that will save his life, marries an ugly hag. The Sibyl was a prophetess to whom Apollo granted as many years of life as the number of grains of sand she could hold. Xanthippe was the notoriously shrewish wife of Socrates.

6 *or a worse*

Or someone even worse

7 *She moves me not, or not removes at least / Affection's edge*

She doesn't bother me, or at least doesn't prevent my eagerness to have her.

Hortensio

guarantor   Petruchio, patience. I am Grumio's pledge.°

Why, this' a heavy chance[1] 'twixt him and you,

long-standing/witty   Your ancient,° trusty, pleasant° servant Grumio.

And tell me now, sweet friend, what happy gale[2]   45

Blows you to Padua here from old Verona?

Petruchio

Such wind as scatters young men through the world

To seek their fortunes farther than at home,

little/i.e., few words   Where small° experience grows. But, in a few,°

Signior Hortensio, thus it stands with me: 50

Antonio, my father, is deceased,

i.e., complex world   And I have thrust myself into this maze,°

marry   Happily to wive° and thrive as best I may.

Coins   Crowns° in my purse I have and goods at home,

And so am come abroad to see the world.   55

Hortensio

Petruchio, shall I then come roundly to[3] thee

shrewish/ill-tempered   And wish thee to a shrewd,° ill-favored° wife?

advice   Thou'dst thank me but a little for my counsel.°

And yet I'll promise thee she shall be rich,

And very rich. But thou'rt too much my friend,   60

And I'll not wish thee to her.

Petruchio

Signior Hortensio, 'twixt such friends as we

Few words suffice. And therefore, if thou know

One rich enough to be Petruchio's wife,

As wealth is burden[4] of my wooing dance,   65

ugly   Be she as foul° as was Florentius' love,

ill-tempered   As old as Sibyl, and as curst° and shrewd

As Socrates' Xanthippe,[5] or a worse,[6]

She moves me not, or not removes at least

Affection's edge[7] in me, were she as rough   70

1   *aglet-baby*

     I.e., doll. An *aglet* was a tiny figure
     carved as an ornament for the end
     of a cord or lace.

2   *are stepped thus far in*

     Have gone this far

3   *that I broached*

     What I began

4   *board her*

     Woo her. (Petruchio uses an image
     of sailors boarding an enemy ship
     in battle. *Board her* also can mean
     "mount her" in the sexual sense.)

As are the swelling Adriatic seas.

I come to wive it wealthily in Padua,

If wealthily, then happily in Padua.

Grumio

frankly [*to* **Hortensio**] Nay, look you, sir, he tells you flatly°

what his mind is. Why, give him gold enough and   75

hag marry him to a puppet or an aglet-baby, ¹ or an old trot°

with ne'er a tooth in her head, though she have as

many diseases as two-and-fifty horses. Why, nothing

with it comes amiss, so money comes withal. °

Hortensio

Petruchio, since we are stepped thus far in, ²   80

I will continue that I broached ³ in jest.

I can, Petruchio, help thee to a wife

With wealth enough, and young and beauteous,

Brought up as best becomes a gentlewoman.

Her only fault, and that is faults enough,   85

intolerably Is that she is intolerable° curst,

shrewish / willful And shrewd° and froward,° so beyond all measure

financial condition That, were my state° far worser than it is,

I would not wed her for a mine of gold.

Petruchio

Hortensio, peace. Thou know'st not gold's effect.   90

Tell me her father's name, and 'tis enough,

scold For I will board her, ⁴ though she chide° as loud

As thunder when the clouds in autumn crack.

Hortensio

Her father is Baptista Minola,

An affable and courteous gentleman.   95

Her name is Katherina Minola,

Renowned in Padua for her scolding tongue.

Petruchio

I know her father, though I know not her,

1   *To give you over at this first encounter*

     To leave you here and now

2   *while the humor lasts*

     While he's in the mood

3   *half a score knaves*

     **Ten different kinds of knave (i.e.,
     many bad names)**

4   *an he begin once*

     If he gets started

5   *rail in his rope tricks*

     **This line has never been satisfac-
     torily explained. *Rope tricks* may be
     Grumio's mistake for "rhetorics"
     (i.e., Petruchio's argumentative
     skills) or it may mean "behavior
     that will be punished by hanging."
     In any case, the idea is that Petru-
     chio will be even more outrageous
     than Katherine.**

6   *stand him*

     **Stand up to him, but also "give him
     an erection"**

7   *throw a figure in her face*

     **Toss a figure of speech at her,
     though possibly with a lost sexual
     innuendo**

8   *disfigure*

     **Both "leave her speechless" (i.e.,
     without figures of speech) and "mar
     her appearance"**

9   *no more eyes to see withal than a cat*

     **I.e., she will be blinded (by his stun-
     ning wit). It is not clear why Grumio
     seems to suggest that cats are blind
     (perhaps the idea is of two cats
     scratching at each other's eyes).**

10   *other more*

     Others as well

11   *before rehearsed*

     Previously recited

And he knew my deceasèd father well.

I will not sleep, Hortensio, till I see her,   100

frank   And therefore let me be thus bold° with you

To give you over at this first encounter, [1]

there   Unless you will accompany me thither.°

Grumio

[*to* **Hortensio**] I pray you, sir, let him go while the

if   humor lasts.[2] O' my word, an° she knew him as well as I   105

do, she would think scolding would do little good upon

him. She may perhaps call him half a score knaves[3] or

rant   so. Why, that's nothing; an he begin once,[4] he'll rail° in

his rope tricks.[5] I'll tell you what, sir: an she stand him[6]

but a little, he will throw a figure in her face[7] and so   110

disfigure[8] her with it that she shall have no more eyes

to see withal than a cat.[9] You know him not, sir.

Hortensio

Wait   Tarry,° Petruchio; I must go with thee,

control   For in Baptista's keep° my treasure is.

custody   He hath the jewel of my life in hold,°   115

His youngest daughter, beautiful Bianca;

And her withholds from me and other more,[10]

Suitors to her and rivals in my love,

Supposing it a thing impossible,

Because of   For° those defects I have before rehearsed,[11]   120

That ever Katherina will be wooed.

taken out; decreed   Therefore this order hath Baptista ta'en:°

That none shall have access unto Bianca

Till Katherine the curst have got a husband.

Grumio

"Katherine the curst!"—   125

A title for a maid of all titles the worst.

Hortensio

a favor   Now shall my friend Petruchio do me grace°

1   *leave and leisure*

     Permission and time

2   *A proper stripling, and an amorous.*

     **A handsome young man (i.e.,
     Lucentio, dressed as Cambio) and
     an amorous one (i.e., Gremio)**

3   *the note*

     I.e., the list of the books

4   *See that at any hand*

     See to that in any case

5   *Over and beside*

     Above and beyond

6   *I'll mend it with a largess*

     **I'll add to it with a financial
     contribution.**

7   *stand you so assured*

     You can be confident

And offer me disguised in sober robes
To old Baptista as a schoolmaster

qualified Well seen° in music, to instruct Bianca,   *130*

plan That so I may, by this device° at least,

speak of; profess Have leave and leisure[1] to make° love to her

And, unsuspected, court her by herself.

Grumio

dishonesty (ironic) Here's no knavery!° See, to beguile the old folks, how
the young folks lay their heads together!   *135*

Enter **Gremio** *and* **Lucentio**, *disguised [as* **Cambio**].

Master, master, look about you. Who goes there, ha?

Hortensio

Peace, Grumio. It is the rival of my love.

Petruchio, stand by a while.

[**Petruchio**, **Hortensio**, *and* **Grumio** *stand aside.*]

Grumio

[*aside*] A proper stripling, and an amorous.[2]

Gremio

[*to* **Lucentio**] Oh, very well, I have perused the note.[3]   *140*

handsomely Hark you, sir: I'll have them very fairly° bound,

All books of love. See that at any hand,[4]

And see you read no other lectures to her.

You understand me? Over and beside[5]

generosity Signior Baptista's liberality,°   *145*

I'll mend it with a largess.[6] Take your paper too,

i.e., the books And let me have them° very well perfumed,

For she is sweeter than perfume itself

i.e., Bianca To whom° they go to. What will you read to her?

Lucentio

Whate'er I read to her, I'll plead for you   *150*

benefactor As for my patron,° stand you so assured,[7]

1   *as yourself were still in place*

As if you were always present

2   *woodcock*

**A bird known for being easy to trap,
and therefore proverbially gullible**

3   *Trow you whither*

Do you know where

4   *no whit*

Not a bit

5   *speak me fair*

Speak civilly to me.

as if As firmly as° yourself were still in place, [1]
Yea, and perhaps with more successful words
Than you, unless you were a scholar, sir.

Gremio

O this learning, what a thing it is!   155

Grumio

[*aside*] O this woodcock, [2] what an ass it is!

Petruchio

[*aside*] Peace, sirrah!

Hortensio

be quiet [*aside*] Grumio, mum!° [*coming forward*] God save you,
Signior Gremio.

Gremio

And you are well met, Signior Hortensio.
Trow you whither [3] I am going? To Baptista Minola.   160
I promised to enquire carefully
About a schoolmaster for the fair Bianca,
And by good fortune I have lighted well
On this young man, for learning and behavior
needs Fit for her turn,° well read in poetry   165
guarantee And other books—good ones, I warrant° ye.

Hortensio

'Tis well. And I have met a gentleman
Hath promised me to help me to another,
A fine musician to instruct our mistress.
So shall I no whit [4] be behind in duty   170
To fair Bianca, so beloved of me.

Gremio

Beloved of me, and that my deeds shall prove.

Grumio

moneybags [*aside*] And that his bags° shall prove.

Hortensio

express Gremio, 'tis now no time to vent° our love.
Listen to me, and, if you speak me fair, [5]   175

1 *indifferent good for either*

   Equally good for both of us

2 *Upon agreement from us to his liking*

   (Who), if we offer him a deal he likes

3 *So said, so done, is well.*

   **What you said—if it can actually be
   done—is good.**

4 *What countryman?*

   Where are you from?

5 *lives for me*

   Exists for my use

6 *But if you have a stomach, to 't, i' God's
   name*

   **But if you are so inclined, do it, for
   God's sake.**

7 *Will I live?*

   I.e., of course!

8 *but to that intent*

   Except for that purpose

I'll tell you news indifferent good for either. [1]
Here is a gentleman whom by chance I met,
Upon agreement from us to his liking, [2]

        [**Petruchio**, *with* **Grumio**, *comes forward.*]

Will undertake to woo curst Katherine,

satisfies him   Yea, and to marry her, if her dowry please. °   180

Gremio

So said, so done, is well. [3]
Hortensio, have you told him all her faults?

Petruchio

I know she is an irksome brawling scold.
If that be all, masters, I hear no harm.

Gremio

No? Say'st me so, friend? What countryman? [4]   185

Petruchio

Born in Verona, old Antonio's son.
My father dead, my fortune lives for me, [5]
And I do hope good days and long to see.

Gremio

would be   O sir, such a life with such a wife were ° strange!
But if you have a stomach, to 't, i' God's name; [6]   190
You shall have me assisting you in all.
But will you woo this wildcat?

Petruchio

                    Will I live? [7]

Grumio

Will he woo her? Ay, or I'll hang her.

Petruchio

Why came I hither but to that intent? [8]

racket/oppress   Think you a little din ° can daunt ° mine ears?   195
Have I not in my time heard lions roar?
Have I not heard the sea, puffed up with winds,

heated up   Rage like an angry boar chafèd ° with sweat?

1   *That gives not half so great a blow to hear /*
     As will a chestnut in a farmer's fire

     **That makes a noise not even half
     as loud as the sound of a roasting
     chestnut bursting**

2   *Fear boys with bugs.*

     Scare boys with bogeymen.

3   brave

     **Well-dressed (i.e., disguised as
     Lucentio)**

cannon Have I not heard great ordnance° in the field,
And Heaven's artillery thunder in the skies?   200
raging Have I not in a pitchèd° battle heard
alarums (calls to arms) Loud 'larums,° neighing steeds, and trumpets' clang?
And do you tell me of a woman's tongue
That gives not half so great a blow to hear
As will a chestnut in a farmer's fire?[1]   205
Tush, tush! Fear boys with bugs.[2]

Grumio
                                    For he fears none.

Gremio
Hortensio, hark.
fortunately This gentleman is happily° arrived,
My mind presumes, for his own good and yours.

Hortensio
I promised we would be contributors   210
expenses And bear his charge° of wooing, whatsoe'er.

Gremio
And so we will, provided that he win her.

Grumio
I would I were as sure of a good dinner.

Enter **Tranio** *brave,*[3] *and* **Biondello**.

Tranio
Gentlemen, God save you. If I may be bold,
beg / quickest Tell me, I beseech° you, which is the readiest° way   215
To the house of Signior Baptista Minola?

Biondello
He that has the two fair daughters? Is 't he you mean?

Tranio
Even he, Biondello.

Gremio
Hark you, sir, you mean not her to—

1   *him and her*

I.e., Baptista and his daughter

2   *What have you to do?*

What business is it of yours?

3   *at any hand*

In any case

4   *get you hence*

Get away from here.

5   *all unknown*

A complete stranger

Tranio

Perhaps him and her, [1] sir. What have you to do? [2]   220

Petruchio

scolds Not her that chides, ° sir, at any hand, [3] I pray.

Tranio

I love no chiders, sir. Biondello, let's away.

Lucentio

[*aside to* **Tranio**] Well begun, Tranio.

Hortensio

Sir, a word ere you go.

Are you a suitor to the maid you talk of, yea or no?

Tranio

And if I be, sir, is it any offense?   225

Gremio

No, if without more words you will get you hence. [4]

Tranio

Why, sir, I pray, are not the streets as free

For me as for you?

Gremio

But so is not she.

Tranio

For what reason, I beseech you?

Gremio

For this reason, if you'll know: 230

chosen That she's the choice° love of Signior Gremio.

Hortensio

That she's the chosen of Signior Hortensio.

Tranio

Wait Softly, ° my masters. If you be gentlemen,

Do me this right: hear me with patience.

Baptista is a noble gentleman,   235

To whom my father is not all unknown, [5]

And, were his daughter fairer than she is,

1 *Leda's daughter*

I.e., Helen of Troy, described in classical mythology as the most beautiful woman in the world

2 *one more*

I.e., one more than she now has

3 *Paris*

Helen of Troy's lover; his abduction of Helen from her husband Menelaus incited the Trojan War.

4 *speed alone*

Be the only winner

5 *give him head*

I.e., give him free rein (as one might give a horse)

6 *let her go by*

Forget about her.

7 *Yea, leave that labor to great Hercules*

Hercules, the son of Zeus and the mortal Alcmena, as punishment for killing his wife and children was assigned to perform *twelve* labors, deemed impossible for mortal men. Gremio sarcastically refers to the wooing and wedding of Katherina as a similarly impossible task. The lines mark an emerging rivalry between Gremio and Petruchio in terms of age and masculinity.

8 *Alcides' twelve*

The *twelve* labors of Hercules (see note 7). Alcides was another name for Hercules derived from the name of one of his ancestors, Alcaeus.

9 *in sooth*

Truly

She may more suitors have, and me for one.
Fair Leda's daughter[1] had a thousand wooers;
Then well one more[2] may fair Bianca have,   240
And so she shall. Lucentio shall make one,

Even if   Though° Paris[3] came in hope to speed alone.[4]

Gremio
What, this gentleman will out-talk us all.

Lucentio
worn-out horse   Sir, give him head;[5] I know he'll prove a jade. °

Petruchio
purpose   Hortensio, to what end° are all these words?   245

Hortensio
[*to* **Tranio**] Sir, let me be so bold as ask you,
Did you yet ever see Baptista's daughter?

Tranio
No, sir, but hear I do that he hath two:
The one as famous for a scolding tongue
As is the other for beauteous modesty.   250

Petruchio
Sir, sir, the first's for me; let her go by.[6]

Gremio
Yea, leave that labor to great Hercules,[7]
And let it be more than Alcides'[8] twelve.

Petruchio
[*to* **Tranio**] Sir, understand you this of me, in sooth:[9]
inquire   The youngest daughter, whom you hearken° for,   255
Her father keeps from all access of suitors
And will not promise her to any man
Until the elder sister first be wed.
The younger then is free, and not before.

Tranio
If it be so, sir, that you are the man   260
help   Must stead° us all, and me amongst the rest,

1   *whose hap*

     He whose fortune

2   *rest generally beholding*

     Are without exception indebted

3   *quaff carouses*

     Drink toasts

4   *as adversaries do in law*

     As rival lawyers do

5   ben venuto

     **I.e., host; *Ben venuto* is Italian for
     "welcome."**

And if you break the ice and do this feat—
Achieve the elder, set the younger free
For our access—whose hap¹ shall be to have her

ungrateful   Will not so graceless be to be ingrate.°   265

Hortensio

understand   Sir, you say well, and well you do conceive,°
And since you do profess to be a suitor,

reward   You must, as we do, gratify ° this gentleman,
To whom we all rest generally beholding.²

Tranio

lacking   Sir, I shall not be slack;° in sign whereof,   270

spend time   Please ye we may contrive° this afternoon
And quaff carouses³ to our mistress' health
And do as adversaries do in law, ⁴

Compete   Strive° mightily, but eat and drink as friends.

Grumio and Biondello

proposal   O excellent motion! ° Fellows, let's be gone.   275

Hortensio

The motion's good indeed, and be it so.
—Petruchio, I shall be your *ben venuto*.⁵   *They exit.*

1   *bondmaid*

Female serf or slave (Bianca is, of course, literally bound, i.e., tied up)

Act 2, Scene 1

Enter **Katherina** *and* **Bianca**, *[her hands tied]*.

Bianca

Good sister, wrong me not, nor wrong yourself,

To make a bondmaid¹ and a slave of me.

articles (of clothing)   That I disdain. But, for these other goods,°

If you unbind   Unbind° my hands, I'll pull them off myself,

clothing   Yea, all my raiment° to my petticoat,   5

Or what you will command me will I do,

So well I know my duty to my elders.

Katherina

Of all thy suitors here I charge thee tell

lie; deceive me   Whom thou lov'st best. See thou dissemble° not.

Bianca

Believe me, sister, of all the men alive   10

I never yet beheld that special face

love   Which I could fancy° more than any other.

Katherina

Brat   Minion,° thou liest. Is 't not Hortensio?

Bianca

like   If you affect° him, sister, here I swear

i.e., but somehow   I'll plead for you myself, but° you shall have him.   15

Katherina

perhaps / desire   Oh, then belike° you fancy° riches more.

well dressed   You will have Gremio to keep you fair.°

Bianca

hate   Is it for him you do envy° me so?

Nay, then you jest, and now I well perceive

You have but jested with me all this while.   20

I prithee, sister Kate, untie my hands.

                 *[**Katherina**] strikes her.*

1   *Whence grows this insolence?*

What is the reason for this con-
temptuous behavior?

2   *ply thy needle*

Work on your embroidery.

3   *For shame, thou hilding of a devilish
spirit!*

Calling Katherina a "hilding" (a
vicious beast, usually used to refer
to an unbroken or bad-tempered
horse) and pointing to her "devilish spirit," Baptista conflates two
dominant patterns of imagery
associated with her throughout
the play. Katherina is frequently
described as an uncontrolled
animal, but the image of a horse
appears several times to suggest
that she will and should be ridden
and tamed, with all the sexual and
domestic implications of those
metaphoric constructions. She is
also frequently associated with
the devil and witchcraft. Although
belief in witches was widespread,
the skeptic Reginald Scot notes in
The Discovery of Witchcraft (1584) that
outspoken or socially disorderly
women might be accused of witchcraft on the assumption that their
troublesome behavior had to have
a supernatural explanation.

4   *suffer me*

Let me have my way

5   *dance barefoot on her wedding day*

The traditional fate of unmarried
elder sisters

6   *lead apes in Hell*

Unmarried women were proverbially said to spend eternity leading
apes into Hell (because they could
not lead children into Heaven).

Katherina

If that be jest, then all the rest was so.

Enter **Baptista**.

Baptista

Why, how now, dame! Whence grows this insolence? [1]
—Bianca, stand aside.—Poor girl, she weeps!
[*unties her hands*] Go ply thy needle; [2] meddle not with
   her.   25
[*to* **Katherina**] For shame, thou hilding of a devilish
   spirit! [3]
Why dost thou wrong her that did ne'er wrong thee?

provoke When did she cross° thee with a bitter word?

Katherina

mocks Her silence flouts° me, and I'll be revenged.

                                          [*She*] *flies after* **Bianca**.

Baptista

What, in my sight?—Bianca, get thee in.   30

                                                    [**Bianca**] *exits*.

Katherina

What, will you not suffer me? [4] Nay, now I see
She is your treasure. She must have a husband;
I must dance barefoot on her wedding day [5]

because of And, for° your love to her, lead apes in Hell. [6]
Talk not to me. I will go sit and weep   35
Till I can find occasion of revenge.   [*She exits.*]

Baptista

troubled; afflicted Was ever gentleman thus grieved° as I?
But who comes here?

1   in the habit of a mean man

Dressed like a poor man

2   *Give me leave.*

Pardon me; let me explain myself.

3   *for an entrance to my entertainment*

As a sign of gratitude for my reception (at your house)

Enter **Gremio**; **Lucentio** [*disguised as* **Cambio**]
in the habit of a mean man; [1] **Petruchio** *with*
[**Hortensio** *disguised as* **Litio**, *a musician, and*]
Tranio [*disguised as* **Lucentio**,] *with his boy*
[**Biondello**,] *bearing a lute and books.*

Gremio

morning   Good morrow,° neighbor Baptista.

Baptista

Good morrow, neighbor Gremio. God save you,   40
gentlemen!

Petruchio

And you, good sir. Pray, have you not a daughter
Called Katherina, fair and virtuous?

Baptista

I have a daughter, sir, called Katherina.

Gremio

properly   [*to* **Petruchio**] You are too blunt. Go to it orderly.°   45

Petruchio

You wrong me, Signior Gremio. Give me leave. [2]
[*to* **Baptista**] I am a gentleman of Verona, sir,

intelligence   That hearing of her beauty and her wit,°
Her affability and bashful modesty,
Her wondrous qualities and mild behavior,   50

eager   Am bold to show myself a forward° guest
Within your house, to make mine eye the witness

often   Of that report which I so oft° have heard.
And, for an entrance to my entertainment, [3]

servant   I do present you with a man° of mine,   55

               [*presenting* **Hortensio**, *disguised as* **Litio**]
Cunning in music and the mathematics,

subjects   To instruct her fully in those sciences,°
Whereof I know she is not ignorant.

1   *Accept of*

    Accept

2   *She is not for your turn, the more my grief*

    **She is not suitable for you, I am
sorry to say.**

3   *like not of*

    Do not like

4   *Whence are you*

    Where are you from

5   *poor petitioners*

    **Seekers after Bianca's love. (Gremio
adopts the conventional rhetoric of
humility expected of a suitor.)**

6   Bacare

    **Step back (pseudo-Latin). Gremio
uses the word in light of his description of Petruchio as "marvelous
forward." In his rivalry with Petruchio, Gremio seems to suggest that
the younger man, like Katherina,
fails to know his place.**

7   *I would fain be doing*

    **I just want to get on with it (with a
pun on *doing* meaning "having sex,"
hinting at Gremio's impotency).**

8   *kindly beholding*

    Naturally attractive

9   *Rheims*

    **A city in northern France with a
renowned university**

Accept of[1] him, or else you do me wrong.

His name is Litio, born in Mantua.   60

Baptista

You're welcome, sir, and he for your good sake.

But for my daughter Katherine, this I know:

She is not for your turn, the more my grief.[2]

Petruchio

I see you do not mean to part with her,

Or else you like not of[3] my company.   65

Baptista

Mistake me not. I speak but as I find.

Whence are you,[4] sir? What may I call your name?

Petruchio

Petruchio is my name, Antonio's son,

A man well known throughout all Italy.

Baptista

I know him well. You are welcome for his sake.   70

Gremio

With all respect to Saving° your tale, Petruchio, I pray

Let us that are poor petitioners[5] speak too.

pushy Bacare,[6] you are marvelous forward.°

Petruchio

Oh, pardon me, Signior Gremio; I would fain be doing.[7]

Gremio

I doubt it not, sir, but you will curse your wooing.   75

gracious [*to* **Baptista**] Neighbor, this is a gift very grateful,° I am

sure of it. To express the like kindness, myself, that

have been more kindly beholding[8] to you than any,

freely give unto you this young scholar [*presenting*

Lucentio, *disguised as* **Cambio**] that hath been long   80

studying at Rheims,[9] as cunning in Greek, Latin, and

other languages as the other in music and mathe-

matics. His name is Cambio. Pray accept his service.

1   *walk like a stranger*

     Are not one of the group

2   *In the preferment of*

     In giving precedence to

3   *free access and favor as the rest*

     **Access (to Bianca) and permission
     (to woo), as the others have**

4   *Lucentio is your name?*

     **Tranio has not told Baptista his
     assumed name; in some produc-
     tions, Baptista reads the name
     Lucentio off one of the books he
     has just received; in others, Tranio
     presents a business card.**

Baptista

A thousand thanks, Signior Gremio. Welcome, good
Cambio. [to **Tranio**] But, gentle sir, methinks you walk   85
like a stranger.[1] May I be so bold to know the cause of
your coming?

Tranio

Pardon me, sir, the boldness is mine own,
That, being a stranger in this city here,
Do make myself a suitor to your daughter,   90
Unto Bianca, fair and virtuous.
Nor is your firm resolve unknown to me
In the preferment of[2] the eldest sister.
This liberty is all that I request,
That, upon knowledge of my parentage,   95
I may have welcome 'mongst the rest that woo
And free access and favor as the rest.[3]
And toward the education of your daughters

i.e., a lute I here bestow a simple instrument°
And this small packet of Greek and Latin books.   100

                         [**Biondello** *presents the gifts.*]

If you accept them, then their worth is great.

Baptista

Lucentio is your name?[4] Of whence, I pray?

Tranio

Of Pisa, sir, son to Vincentio.

Baptista

A mighty man of Pisa. By report
I know him well. You are very welcome, sir.   105
[to **Hortensio**] Take you the lute, [to **Lucentio**] and you
       the set of books.

right away You shall go see your pupils presently.°
—Holla, within!

1   *What dowry shall I have with her to wife*

      See **LONGER NOTE** on page 294.

2   *in possession*

      I.e., immediately to be given her

3   *widowhood*

      I.e., her legal rights as my widow

4   *be it*

      If it happens

5   *on either hand*

      On both our parts

Enter a servant.

                Sirrah, lead these gentlemen
To my daughters and tell them both

treat   These are their tutors. Bid them use° them well.   110

      [*The servant exits with* **Lucentio** *and* **Hortensio**,

          and **Biondello** *following.*]

garden   We will go walk a little in the orchard,°

exceedingly   And then to dinner. You are passing° welcome,

And so I pray you all to think yourselves.

Petruchio

requires   Signior Baptista, my business asketh° haste,

And every day I cannot come to woo.   115

You knew my father well and in him me,

Left solely heir to all his lands and goods,

increased   Which I have bettered° rather than decreased.

Then tell me, if I get your daughter's love,

What dowry shall I have with her to wife?[1]   120

Baptista

After my death, the one half of my lands,

And, in possession,[2] twenty thousand crowns.

Petruchio

And, for that dowry, I'll assure her of

Her widowhood,[3] be it[4] that she survive me,

In all my lands and leases whatsoever.   125

contracts   Let specialties° be therefore drawn between us

agreements   That covenants° may be kept on either hand.[5]

Baptista

Ay, when the special thing is well obtained—

That is, her love, for that is all in all.

1   *happy be thy speed*

May you have good success (*speed*)

2   *to the proof*

**I.e., so as to be invulnerable (*proof*
armor was specially tested to
ensure its strength)**

3   *That shakes not*

**I.e., the mountains shake not (the
use of an apparently singular verb
with a plural subject was not un-
common in early modern English)**

4   *prove*

**Become; turn out to be (with a play
on *prove* meaning "test")**

5   *hold with*

Withstand

6   *mistook her frets*

**Frets are the bars on a lute's neck
that guide a musician's fingering.
Katherina's reported response in
line 152 puns on *frets* meaning
"irritations."**

Petruchio

Why, that is nothing. For I tell you, father,   130

domineering   I am as peremptory° as she proud-minded,

And where two raging fires meet together

They do consume the thing that feeds their fury.

Though little fire grows great with little wind,

Yet extreme gusts will blow out fire and all.   135

i.e., I will behave   So I° to her, and so she yields to me,

For I am rough and woo not like a babe.

Baptista

Well mayst thou woo, and happy be thy speed, [1]

prepared   But be thou armed° for some unhappy words.

Petruchio

Ay, to the proof, [2] as mountains are for winds   140

That shakes not [3] though they blow perpetually.

                   Enter **Hortensio** [*disguised as* **Litio**], *with his head*

injured   *broke.°*

Baptista

How now, my friend, why dost thou look so pale?

Hortensio

For fear, I promise you, if I look pale.

Baptista

What, will my daughter prove [4] a good musician?

Hortensio

I think she'll sooner prove a soldier.   145

Iron may hold with [5] her, but never lutes.

Baptista

train / i.e., to play   Why, then thou canst not break° her to° the lute?

Hortensio

on   Why, no, for she hath broke the lute to° me.

I did but tell her she mistook her frets [6]

bent   And bowed° her hand to teach her fingering,   150

1   *fume with*

     (1) be furious at; (2) be furious using

2   *pillory*

     Wooden frame that secured a
     criminal's head and arms, either for
     a whipping or as a form of public
     humiliation

3   *As had she*

     As if she had

When, with a most impatient devilish spirit,
"'Frets' call you these?" quoth she. "I'll fume with ¹
    them!"
And with that word she struck me on the head,
skull   And through the instrument my pate° made way,
And there I stood amazèd for awhile,   155
As on a pillory, ² looking through the lute,
While she did call me "rascal fiddler"
knave   And "twangling jack,"° with twenty such vile terms
As had she ³ studied to misuse me so.

Petruchio

spirited; lively   Now, by the world, it is a lusty° wench.   160
I love her ten times more than e'er I did.
Oh, how I long to have some chat with her!

Baptista

[*to* **Hortensio**] Well, go with me and be not so
discouraged   discomfited.°
Proceed in practice with my younger daughter.
favors   She's apt to learn and thankful for good turns.°   165
Signior Petruchio, will you go with us,
Or shall I send my daughter Kate to you?

Petruchio

wait for   I pray you do. I'll attend° her here.

                      Petruchio *remains;* [*the others*] *exit.*

And woo her with some spirit when she comes.
rant / plainly   Say that she rail,° why then I'll tell her plain°   170
She sings as sweetly as a nightingale.
serene   Say that she frown, I'll say she looks as clear°
As morning roses newly washed with dew.
Say she be mute and will not speak a word,
fluency in speech   Then I'll commend her volubility°   175
poignant; moving   And say she uttereth piercing° eloquence.
leave   If she do bid me pack,° I'll give her thanks

1   *ask the banns*

Elizabethan marriages were preceded by a public reading of the *banns* (a formal announcement of an impending wedding) normally at three consecutive Sunday church services.

2   *hard of hearing*

Hard puns on *heard* earlier in the line, as the two were pronounced the same way in early modern English.

3   *for you are called plain Kate*

See LONGER NOTE on page 295.

4   *Kate Hall*

Perhaps a reference to Katherine Hall, a large house in southern England, or some other specific place; most likely, however, an ironic way of saying "the house that Kate is in charge of."

5   *dainties are all Kates*

Punning on the fact that both *dainties* and "cates," refer to small cakes or candies

6   *sounded*

"Proclaimed," but also "checked for depth" (as one *sounds* the bottom of the ocean), an image Petruchio continues in the following line with the word "deeply"

7   *at the first*

From the start

8   *moveable*

Punning on two senses: "a piece of furniture" and "an inconstant person"

9   *A joint stool.*

A stool made of several separate pieces skillfully joined together

10   *Thou hast hit it.*

There you have it.

As though she bid me stay by her a week.

beg for   If she deny to wed, I'll crave° the day

When I shall ask the banns[1] and when be marrièd.   *180*

Enter **Katherina**.

But here she comes—and now, Petruchio, speak.

Good morrow, Kate—for that's your name, I hear.

Katherina

Well have you heard, but something hard of hearing.[2]

They call me Katherine that do talk of me.

Petruchio

You lie, in faith, for you are called plain Kate,[3]   *185*

i.e., plump   And bonny° Kate, and sometimes Kate the curst;

But Kate, the prettiest Kate in Christendom,

Kate of Kate Hall,[4] my super-dainty Kate—

For dainties are all Kates[5]—and therefore, Kate,

comfort   Take this of me, Kate of my consolation:°   *190*

gentleness   Hearing thy mildness° praised in every town,

Thy virtues spoke of, and thy beauty sounded[6]

(Yet not so deeply as to thee belongs)

Myself am moved to woo thee for my wife.

Katherina

"Moved," in good time. Let him that moved you hither   *195*

Remove you hence. I knew you at the first[7]

You were a moveable.[8]

Petruchio

                  Why, what's a moveable?

Katherina

A joint stool.[9]

Petruchio

                Thou hast hit it.[10] Come sit on me.

1　*bear*

Katherina uses the word to mean
"carry loads," but Petruchio in the
next line plays on the senses "give
birth to children" and "bear the
weight of a man during intercourse."

2　*jade*

An old, tired horse (an insult aimed
at Petruchio's stamina as a lover)

3　*burden thee*

(1) burden you with my weight (during intercourse); (2) accuse you

4　*For knowing*

Since I know

5　*light*

(1) promiscuous; (2) not heavy; (3) of
little importance

6　*as heavy as my weight should be*

Katherina's punning adds to the
literal sense (1) "as respectable as
someone of my status should be";
(2) "as valuable as possible," playing on coinage: clipped coins were
light; i.e., had fewer grains of silver
or gold than in coins of proper
weight.

7　*should buzz*

Buzz is both the sound made by a
bee (playing on "be" earlier in the
line) as well as a term meaning "ru-
mor or scandal." Thus, Petruchio

either expresses his impatience
at Katherina's buzzing chatter or
implies that she deserves to be the
subject of gossip (or, perhaps, has
already been so).

8　*buzzard*

I.e., a dull, stupid person (perhaps
since buzzards could not be trained
for hawking)

9　*turtle*

Turtledove, a symbol of fidelity

10　*Ay, for a turtle, as he takes a buzzard.*

Unclear; perhaps, if you take me
as your wife because you think I'll
be faithful, I'll turn on you like a
turtledove swallowing a buzzing
insect (*buzzard*).

Katherina

Asses are made to bear,[1] and so are you.

Petruchio

Women are made to bear, and so are you.   200

Katherina

No such jade[2] as you, if me you mean.

Petruchio

Alas, good Kate, I will not burden thee,[3]

For knowing[4] thee to be but young and light[5]—

Katherina

quick-witted / country boy Too light° for such a swain° as you to catch,

And yet as heavy as my weight should be.[6]   205

Petruchio

"Should be"—should buzz![7]

Katherina

taken (caught in flight)   Well ta'en,° and like a buzzard.[8]

Petruchio

O slow-winged turtle,[9] shall a buzzard take thee?

Katherina

Ay, for a turtle, as he takes a buzzard.[10]

Petruchio

Come, come, you wasp. I' faith, you are too angry.

Katherina

If I be waspish, best beware my sting.   210

Petruchio

My remedy is then to pluck it out.

Katherina

Ay, if the fool could find it where it lies.

Petruchio

Who knows not where a wasp does wear his sting?

its In his° tail.

Katherina

In his tongue.

1 *tales*

Rumors (with a sexual pun on "tails" that Petruchio makes explicit in line 216)

2 *come again*

I.e, let's start over.

3 *I swear I'll cuff you if you strike again.*

Although men were traditionally authorized to use force against their wives, servants, and children to maintain order in their households, by Shakespeare's time the practice was increasingly discouraged. The impact of Protestant ideas of marriage as a companionate relationship inhibited the use of force. The Elizabethan "Homily of Matrimony," for instance, compared the control of one's wife to the farming of land, whereby the husband/farmer should "diligently apply [himself] to weed out little by little the noisome weeds of uncomely manners out of her mind, with wholesome precepts." Domestic violence, no doubt too facilely, was usually viewed as a marker of lower-class status, so when Petruchio says he is a "gentleman," Katherina decides to test (*try*) his assertion by seeing if he will strike her back.

4 *lose your arms*

In early modern English, *lose* and "loose" were interchangeable, so the phrase means (1) loosen your hold; (2) forfeit your coat of arms.

5 *A herald*

Heralds were responsible for keeping records of the nobility and their respective coats of arms.

6 *put me in thy books*

Both "record my name in your heraldic books" and "take me into your good graces"

7 *coxcomb*

A jester's cap, named for its resemblance to a rooster's crest

8 *combless cock*

A harmless rooster (with a sexual innuendo suggesting a satisfied penis)

9 *craven*

A rooster with no fighting instinct

10 *crab*

Crab apple, a tart, sour fruit; hence, an ill-tempered person

11 *here's no crab*

There's no crab here (i.e., I'm no crab).

Petruchio

                                                    Whose tongue?

Katherina

Yours, if you talk of tales. [1] And so farewell.   215

Petruchio

What, with my tongue in your tail? Nay, come again, [2]
Good Kate. I am a gentleman.

Katherina

test   That I'll try. °

                                              She strikes him.

Petruchio

hit   I swear I'll cuff° you if you strike again. [3]   [*He holds her.*]

Katherina

So may you lose your arms: [4]
If you strike me, you are no gentleman,   220
coat of arms   And if no gentleman, why then no arms. °

Petruchio

A herald, [5] Kate? Oh, put me in thy books! [6]

Katherina

symbol on a coat of arms   What is your crest? ° A coxcomb? [7]

Petruchio

if   A combless cock, [8] so ° Kate will be my hen.

Katherina

too much   No cock of mine. You crow too ° like a craven. [9]   225

Petruchio

Nay, come, Kate, come. You must not look so sour.

Katherina

It is my fashion, when I see a crab. [10]

Petruchio

Why, here's no crab, [11] and therefore look not sour.

Katherina

There is; there is.

1   *Well aimed of*

     Well guessed by

2   *by Saint George*

     **A common oath (*Saint George* is the
     patron saint of England)**

3   *you 'scape not so*

     You won't escape so easily.

4   *I chafe you*

     **I'll annoy you (with a sexual innu-
     endo, i.e., I'll get you excited)**

5   *look askance*

     Scowl

Petruchio

to me   Then show it me.°

Katherina

mirror   Had I a glass,° I would.   230

Petruchio

What? You mean my face?

Katherina

                    Well aimed of¹ such a young one.

Petruchio

vigorous   Now, by Saint George,² I am too young° for you.

Katherina

wrinkled   Yet you are withered.°

Petruchio

                    'Tis with cares.

Katherina

                                        I care not.

Petruchio

listen / truth   Nay, hear° you, Kate: in sooth° you 'scape not so.³

Katherina

stay   I chafe you⁴ if I tarry.° Let me go.   235

Petruchio

bit / surpassingly   No, not a whit.° I find you passing° gentle.

aloof   'Twas told me you were rough and coy° and sullen,

total   And now I find report a very° liar,

playful   For thou art pleasant, gamesome,° passing courteous,

But slow in speech, yet sweet as springtime flowers.   240

Thou canst not frown, thou canst not look askance,⁵

Nor bite the lip as angry wenches will,

confrontational   Nor hast thou pleasure to be cross° in talk;

But thou with mildness entertain'st thy wooers,

conversation   With gentle conference,° soft and affable.   245

Why does the world report that Kate doth limp?

O sland'rous world! Kate, like the hazel-twig,

1   *brown*

   Probably an insult, since fair skin was prized in Elizabethan women

2   *and whom thou keep'st command*

   Give orders to your servants (not to me)

3   *Dian*

   Diana, Roman goddess of chastity

4   *princely gait*

   Noble bearing

5   *It is extempore, from my mother wit.*

   It is spontaneous from my native intelligence.

6   *Witless else her son.*

   I.e., her son would otherwise be brainless.

7   *Keep you warm.*

   To be "wise enough to keep warm" was a proverbial expression used to describe someone of little intelligence.

8   *will you, nill you*

   Whether it is your will or not

9   *for your turn*

   Fit for you

10 *wild Kate*

   I.e., "wildcat" (as *household Kates* in line 271 plays on "household cats")

Is straight and slender and as brown [1] in hue
As hazel nuts, and sweeter than the kernels.

                              [*He lets her go.*]

limp   Oh, let me see thee walk! Thou dost not halt. °   250
Katherina
Go, fool, and whom thou keep'st command. [2]
Petruchio
adorn   Did ever Dian [3] so become° a grove
As Kate this chamber with her princely gait? [4]
Oh, be thou Dian, and let her be Kate,
amorous   And then let Kate be chaste and Dian sportful. °   255
Katherina
impressive   Where did you study all this goodly° speech?
Petruchio
It is extempore, from my mother wit. [5]
Katherina
A witty mother! Witless else her son. [6]
Petruchio
Am I not wise?
Katherina
                  Yes. Keep you warm. [7]
Petruchio
i.e., Indeed / mean to   Marry,° so I mean,° sweet Katherine, in thy bed.   260
And therefore, setting all this chat aside,
Thus in plain terms: your father hath consented
i.e., agreed   That you shall be my wife, your dowry 'greed° on,
And, will you, nill you, [8] I will marry you.
Now, Kate, I am a husband for your turn, [9]   265
For, by this light, whereby I see thy beauty,
Thy beauty that doth make me like thee well,
Thou must be married to no man but me.
i.e., who is   For I am he am° born to tame you, Kate,
And bring you from a wild Kate [10] to a Kate   270
Compliant   Conformable° as other household Kates.

1   *how speed you*

    How are you getting on?

2   *speed amiss*

    Fare poorly

3   *In your dumps?*

    I.e., are you depressed?

4   *That thinks with oaths to face the matter
    out*

    **I.e., who thinks he can get his own
    way by his own brazen insistence**

5   *for policy*

    A tactic

6   *Grissel*

    **Patient *Grissel*, or Griselda, was a
    model of wifely obedience despite
    her abusive husband. Numerous
    versions of the Griselda story ap-
    pear throughout English literature,
    including "The Clerk's Tale" in
    Geoffrey Chaucer's *The Canterbury
    Tales*.**

7   *Lucrece*

    **A classical paragon of chastity, who
    killed herself in despair after hav-
    ing been raped by her brother-in-
    law Tarquin. Shakespeare recounts
    the story in his poem *The Rape of
    Lucrece* (1594).**

Enter **Baptista**, **Gremio**, [*and*] **Tranio** [*disguised as* **Lucentio**].

Here comes your father. Never make denial.
I must and will have Katherine to my wife.

Baptista
Now, Signior Petruchio, how speed you [1] with my
    daughter?

Petruchio
How but well, sir? How but well?   275
It were impossible I should speed amiss. [2]

Baptista
Why, how now, daughter Katherine? In your dumps? [3]

Katherina
Call you me daughter? Now, I promise you,
You have showed a tender fatherly regard
To wish me wed to one half lunatic,   280
knave   A madcap ruffian, and a swearing jack,°
That thinks with oaths to face the matter out. [4]

Petruchio
Father, 'tis thus: yourself and all the world
wrongly   That talked of her have talked amiss° of her.
shrewish   If she be curst,° it is for policy, [5]   285
proud; stubborn   For she's not froward,° but modest as the dove.
hot tempered   She is not hot,° but temperate as the morn.
For patience she will prove a second Grissel, [6]
And Roman Lucrece [7] for her chastity.
i.e., agreed   And, to conclude, we have 'greed° so well together   290
on   That upon° Sunday is the wedding day.

Katherina
I'll see thee hanged on Sunday first.

Gremio
Hark, Petruchio; she says she'll see thee hanged first.

1   *good night our part*

     I.e., that's the end of our hopes.

2   *'twixt us twain*

     Between the two of us

3   *curst in company*

     Quarrelsome when we're in public

4   *'Tis a world to see*

     It's worth all the world to see

5   *fine array*

     Beautiful clothes

6   *clapped up*

     Arranged; agreed upon

Tranio

success   Is this your speeding?° Nay, then, good night our part.[1]

Petruchio

Be patient, gentlemen. I choose her for myself.   295

If she and I be pleased, what's that to you?

'Tis bargained 'twixt us twain,[2] being alone,

That she shall still be curst in company.[3]

I tell you, 'tis incredible to believe

How much she loves me. Oh, the kindest Kate!   300

She hung about my neck, and kiss on kiss

repeated / swearing   She vied° so fast, protesting° oath on oath,

instant   That in a twink° she won me to her love.

amateurs   Oh, you are novices!° 'Tis a world to see[4]

How tame, when men and women are alone,   305

meek / most quarrelsome   A meacock° wretch can make the curstest° shrew.

—Give me thy hand, Kate. I will unto Venice

in preparation for   To buy apparel 'gainst° the wedding day.

invite   Provide the feast, father, and bid° the guests.

well dressed   I will be sure my Katherine shall be fine.°   310

Baptista

I know not what to say, but give me your hands.

God send you joy, Petruchio. 'Tis a match.

Gremio and Tranio

Amen, say we. We will be witnesses.

Petruchio

Father, and wife, and gentlemen, adieu.

quickly   I will to Venice. Sunday comes apace.°   315

We will have rings and things and fine array,[5]

on   And kiss me, Kate. We will be married o'° Sunday.

                         Petruchio *and* **Katherina** *exit.*

Gremio

Was ever match clapped up[6] so suddenly?

1   *venture madly on a desperate mart*

     Invest crazily in a risky venture

2   *lay fretting by you*

     (1) wearing out while you had it;
     (2) that was irritating to you

3   *quiet in the match*

     Peace and quiet, knowing that
     Katherina is engaged

4   *a quiet catch*

     Spoken ironically of Petruchio's
     ***catch*, Katherina.**

5   *fry*

     Burn (because too eager and
     passionate)

6   *Content you*

     Calm down; be content.

7   *compound this strife*

     Settle this quarrel

8   *deeds*

     Actions (but legal *deeds* to property
     will ultimately decide the match)

9   *greatest dower*

     I.e., the largest dowry (see
     2.1.120–124 and LONGER NOTE on
     p. 294)

Baptista

Faith, gentlemen, now I play a merchant's part

And venture madly on a desperate mart. [1]   320

Tranio

'Twas a commodity lay fretting by you. [2]

profit   'Twill bring you gain° or perish on the seas.

Baptista

The gain I seek is quiet in the match. [3]

Gremio

No doubt but he hath got a quiet catch. [4]

But now, Baptista, to your younger daughter.   325

Now is the day we long have lookèd for.

I am your neighbor and was suitor first.

Tranio

And I am one that love Bianca more

Than words can witness or your thoughts can guess.

Gremio

Youngster / dearly   Youngling,° thou canst not love so dear° as I.   330

Tranio

Old man / i.e., shrivel   Graybeard, ° thy love doth freeze.°

Gremio

But thine doth fry. [5]

Flighty youth   Skipper,° stand back. 'Tis age that nourisheth.

Tranio

But youth in ladies' eyes that flourisheth.

Baptista

Content you, [6] gentlemen. I will compound this strife. [7]

i.e., the two of you   'Tis deeds [8] must win the prize, and he of both °   335

That can assure my daughter greatest dower [9]

Shall have my Bianca's love.

Say, Signior Gremio, what can you assure her?

Gremio

First, as you know, my house within the city

1 *Tyrian*

Tyre, a coastal city in modern Lebanon, was famous for its expensive fabric dyes.

2 *arras counterpoints*

Woven bedcovers from Arras, a northern French town famous for its tapestries (in fact, the word *arras* came to be synonymous with "tapestry")

3 *Valance of Venice gold in needlework*

A *valance* was the fringed border around a bed canopy; *Venice gold* refers to an expensive gold thread produced in Venice

4 *milch-kine to the pail*

I.e., cows for milking

5 *answerable to this portion*

Required for such an estate

6 *struck in years*

Old. The image is of coins *struck* (stamped) with the date of their minting.

7 *That "only" came well in.*

I.e., that word "only" serves as the perfect transition to my plea.

8 *by the year / Of fruitful land*

In annual income from my fertile estate

9 *argosy*

The largest type of merchant ship

10 *Marseilles's road*

The protected harbor of Marseilles (the Folio spelling, "Marcellus" revealing the Elizabethan pronunciation)

fine silverware   Is richly furnishèd with plate° and gold,   340

pitchers / wash   Basins and ewers° to lave° her dainty hands,

draperies   My hangings° all of Tyrian [1] tapestry,

chests / coins   In ivory coffers° I have stuffed my crowns,°

In cypress chests my arras counterpoints, [2]

bed curtains   Costly apparel, tents,° and canopies,   345

Turkish / embossed   Fine linen, Turkey° cushions bossed° with pearl,

Valance of Venice gold in needlework, [3]

Pewter and brass, and all things that belongs

To house or housekeeping. Then, at my farm,

I have a hundred milch-kine to the pail, [4]   350

One hundred twenty   Six-score° fat oxen standing in my stalls,

And all things answerable to this portion. [5]

Myself am struck in years, [6] I must confess,

And if I die tomorrow this is hers,

If whilst I live she will be only mine.   355

Tranio

listen   That "only" came well in. [7] Sir, list° to me:

I am my father's heir and only son.

If I may have your daughter to my wife,

I'll leave her houses three or four as good,

Within rich Pisa walls, as any one   360

Old Signior Gremio has in Padua,

gold coins   Besides two thousand ducats° by the year

inheritance   Of fruitful land, [8] all which shall be her jointure. °

distressed   — What, have I pinched° you, Signior Gremio?

Gremio

Two thousand ducats by the year of land?   365

[*aside*] My land amounts not to so much in all.

—That she shall have, besides an argosy [9]

That now is lying in Marseilles's road. [10]

[*to* **Tranio**] What, have I choked you with an argosy?

1   *three great argosies, besides two*
    gallaisses

    **Three large merchant ships, in
    addition to two cargo ships**

2   *tight galleys*

    **Seaworthy trading ships, smaller
    than *galliasses* or *argosies***

3   *the maid is mine from all the world*

    I am the winner over everyone else.

4   *let your father make her the assurance*

    **Provided your father make her his
    heir**

Tranio

Gremio, 'tis known my father hath no less   370
Than three great argosies, besides two galliasses [1]
And twelve tight galleys. [2] These I will assure her,
And twice as much whate'er thou offer'st next.

Gremio

Nay, I have offered all. I have no more,
And she can have no more than all I have.   375
[to **Baptista**] If you like me, she shall have me and mine.

Tranio

Why, then the maid is mine from all the world, [3]
outbid   By your firm promise. Gremio is outvied. °

Baptista

I must confess your offer is the best,
i.e., providing   And, let° your father make her the assurance, [4]   380
otherwise   She is your own; else,° you must pardon me.
If you should die before him, where's her dower?

Tranio

minor problem   That's but a cavil: ° he is old, I young.

Gremio

And may not young men die as well as old?

Baptista

Well, gentlemen, I am thus resolved: 385
On Sunday next, you know,
My daughter Katherine is to be married.
[to **Tranio**] Now, on the Sunday following, shall Bianca
Be bride to you, if you make this assurance.
If not, to Signior Gremio.   390
And so I take my leave and thank you both.

Gremio

Adieu, good neighbor.

                  [**Baptista**] *exits.*
Now I fear thee not.

1   *Set foot under thy table*

   I.e., depend on your charity

2   *a toy*

   I.e., nonsense

3   *faced it with a card of ten*

   A proverbial phrase for "bluffed
   my way through it" (from the card
   game Primero, in which the ten was
   a low-valued card)

4   *supposed*

   I.e., the person thought to be. In
   dramatizing the play's various
   impersonations and disguises—
   that is, the many "supposed"
   characters—that the witty Tranio
   engineers to help Lucentio in his
   pursuit of Bianca, Shakespeare
   adapted material from George
   Gascoigne's play *The Supposes* (1566),
   which was based on Ludovico
   Ariosto's Italian original,
   I Suppositi (1509).

gambler / would be	Sirrah, young gamester,° your father were° a fool
	To give thee all and in his waning age
	Set foot under thy table.[1] Tut, a toy![2] 395
	An old Italian fox is not so kind, my boy. *He exits.*

Tranio

curse	A vengeance° on your crafty withered hide!
	Yet I have faced it with a card of ten.[3]
	'Tis in my head to do my master good.
other way	I see no reason° but supposed[4] Lucentio 400
	Must get a father, called (supposed) Vincentio—
miracle	And that's a wonder.° Fathers commonly
beget	Do get° their children, but, in this case of wooing,
father / with	A child shall get a sire,° if I fail not of° my cunning.

He exits.

1   *wrangling*

   Argumentative

2   *have leisure for as much*

   Be allotted the same amount of
   time

3   *Preposterous*

   Unreasonable; the word literally
   means "putting things first that
   should be last"

4   *usual pain*

   Daily labor

5   *resteth in my choice*

   I.e., is my decision

6   *no breeching scholar in the schools*

   I.e., no child; *breeching* could refer
   either to that moment at about age
   seven when a young boy would first
   be given doublet and hose to wear
   (in contrast to the coats and aprons
   worn by children of either sex) or to
   the practice of flogging school boys
   who failed to learn their lessons.

7   *cut off all strife*

   End all arguing

8   *Take you*

   I.e., pick up

Act 3, Scene 1

Enter **Lucentio** [*disguised as* **Cambio**], **Hortensio**
[*disguised as* **Litio**], *and* **Bianca**.

Lucentio

stop/bold Fiddler, forbear.° You grow too forward,° sir.
reception Have you so soon forgot the entertainment°
with Her sister Katherine welcomed you withal?°

Hortensio

i.e., Bianca But, wrangling[1] pedant, this° is
The patroness of heavenly harmony; 5
Therefore/priority Then° give me leave to have prerogative,°
And when in music we have spent an hour,
lesson Your lecture° shall have leisure for as much.[2]

Lucentio

Preposterous[3] ass, that never read so far
created To know the cause why music was ordained!° 10
Was it not to refresh the mind of man
After his studies or his usual pain?[4]
Then give me leave to read philosophy
bring And, while I pause, serve° in your harmony.

Hortensio

insults Sirrah, I will not bear these braves° of thine. 15

Bianca

Why, gentlemen, you do me double wrong
compete To strive° for that which resteth in my choice.[5]
I am no breeching scholar in the schools.[6]
appointed I'll not be tied to hours nor 'pointed° times
But learn my lessons as I please myself. 20
And, to cut off all strife,[7] here sit we down.
[*to* **Hortensio**] Take you[8] your instrument; play you
meanwhile the whiles.°
before His lecture will be done ere° you have tuned.

153

1   *left we last*

Did we leave off

2   Hic ibat Simois, hic est Sigeia
tellus, / Hic steterat Priami regia
celsa senis.

**Lucentio reads to Bianca from book
1 of Ovid's *Heroides* (circa 1 B.C.),
a series of poems in the form of
fictitious love letters written by legendary women to their husbands or
lovers. Lucentio quotes Penelope's
letter to Odysseus: "Here is where
the Simois used to flow, here is the
Sigeian land, / Here once stood
the lofty palace of aged Priam."
Later, in Act Four, Lucentio will read
to Bianca from Ovid's *Art of Love*
(4.2.8), a verse manual on the art of
seduction. By Shakespeare's time,
Ovid was considered too scandal-
ous to be used in the formal education of young ladies, although the
Latin classics that were introduced
into England by humanist writers
and teachers in the 15th and 16th
centuries themselves provided a far
more frank discussion of love and
sexuality than that to be found in
the native literary tradition.**

3   *bearing my port*

**Assuming my position (i.e., pre-
tending to be me)**

4   *The treble jars.*

I.e., the high notes are out of tune.

5   *Spit in the hole, man, and tune again.*

**Lucentio is probably adapting the
adage "Spit in your hands and take
a better hold" (i.e., "Try again").**

Hortensio

You'll leave his lecture when I am in tune?

Lucentio

That will be never. Tune your instrument.   25

Bianca

Where left we last? [1]

Lucentio

Here, madam:

[*reads*] *Hic ibat Simois, hic est Sigeia tellus,*
Hic steterat Priami regia celsa senis. [2]

Bianca

i.e., Translate Conster° them.   30

Lucentio

Hic ibat—as I told you before; *Simois*—I am Lucentio;
hic est—son unto Vincentio of Pisa; *Sigeia tellus*—
disguised thus to get your love. *Hic steterat*—and that
"Lucentio" that comes a-wooing; *Priami*—is my man
Tranio; *regia*—bearing my port;[3] *celsa senis*—that we   35

crotchety old man might beguile the old pantaloon. °

Hortensio

Madam, my instrument's in tune.

Bianca

Let's hear. [*He plays.*] O fie! The treble jars. [4]

Lucentio

Spit in the hole, man, and tune again.[5]

Bianca

[*to* **Lucentio**] Now let me see if I can conster it. *Hic*   40
ibat Simois—I know you not; *hic est Sigeia tellus*—I trust
you not; *Hic steterat Priami*—take heed he hear us not;
regia—presume not; *celsa senis*—despair not.

Hortensio

Madam, 'tis now in tune.   [*plays again*]

Lucentio

low notes   All but the bass.°

1   *the base knave*

Worthless rascal (i.e., Lucentio)

2   Pedascule

**"Little pedant" (Hortensio invents
this pseudo-Latin phrase,
pronounced as four syllables.)**

3   *For sure Aeacides / Was Ajax, called so
from his grandfather*

**Lucentio quickly returns to his
lesson so as to avoid suspicion.
Aeacides was an alternate name for
the Greek warrior Ajax, given to him
in honor of his grandfather Aeacus.**

4   *give me leave*

Leave us alone.

5   *My lessons make no music in three parts.*

I.e., I have no music for a trio.

6   *fairly drawn*

Clearly written

Hortensio

The bass is right; 'tis the base knave[1] that jars.   45

ardent / teacher   [*aside*] How fiery° and forward our pedant° is!

Now, for my life, the knave doth court my love.

Pedascule,[2] I'll watch you better yet.

Bianca

[*to* **Lucentio**] In time I may believe, yet I mistrust.

Lucentio

[*to* **Bianca**] Mistrust it not. —For sure Aeacides   50

Was Ajax, called so from his grandfather.[3]

Bianca

otherwise   I must believe my master; else,° I promise you,

question   I should be arguing still upon that doubt.°

But let it rest. Now, Litio, to you.

Good master, take it not unkindly, pray,   55

playful   That I have been thus pleasant° with you both.

Hortensio

[*to* **Lucentio**] You may go walk, and give me leave[4]

      awhile.

My lessons make no music in three parts.[5]

Lucentio

Are you so formal, sir? Well, I must wait.

also / unless   [*aside*] And watch withal,° for, but° I be deceived,   60

Our fine musician groweth amorous.

Hortensio

Madam, before you touch the instrument

method   To learn the order° of my fingering,

I must begin with rudiments of art

the musical scale   To teach you gamut° in a briefer sort,   65

concise   More pleasant, pithy,° and effectual

Than hath been taught by any of my trade.

And there it is in writing, fairly drawn.[6]

1   *am past my gamut*

     I.e., have learned my scales

2   *the ground of all accord*

     The basis of all harmony. Both the
     ***ground*, or key note, and the scale**
     itself could be called the *gamut*. The
     notes of a scale (*A, B, C*, etc.) were
     sung on the syllables *re, mi, fa*, etc.,
     as described in Hortensio's lesson.

3   *pry into*

     Investigate

4   *Seize thee that list!*

     Let anyone who wants you take you.

5   *will be quit with thee by changing*

     Will drop you (or "get even with
     you") by finding a new woman

Bianca

Why, I am past my gamut[1] long ago.

Hortensio

Yet read the gamut of Hortensio.   70

Bianca

[*reads*] "Gamut I am, the ground of all accord:[2]

A re, to plead Hortensio's passion;

B mi, Bianca, take him for thy lord;

C fa ut, that loves with all affection;

D sol re, one clef, two notes have I;   75

E la mi, show pity, or I die."

Call you this "gamut"? Tut, I like it not.

fickle Old fashions please me best. I am not so nice°

To change true rules for odd inventions.

Enter a **Messenger**.

Messenger

Mistress, your father prays you leave your books   80

decorate And help to dress° your sister's chamber up.

You know tomorrow is the wedding day.

Bianca

Farewell, sweet masters both. I must be gone.

Lucentio

Faith, mistress, then I have no cause to stay.

[**Bianca**, **Messenger**, *and* **Lucentio** *exit.*]

Hortensio

But I have cause to pry into[3] this pedant.   85

Methinks he looks as though he were in love.

low Yet if thy thoughts, Bianca, be so humble°

bait; decoy To cast thy wand'ring eyes on every stale,°

straying; cheating Seize thee that list![4] If once I find thee ranging,°

Hortensio will be quit with thee by changing.[5]   90

He exits.

1   *we hear not of*

I.e., there is no sign of

2   *noted for*

Regarded as

3   *proclaim the banns*

**Formally announce the intention to
marry (see 2.1.180 and note)**

4   *fortune stays him*

Circumstance keeps him

Act 3, Scene 2

Enter **Baptista**, **Gremio**, **Tranio** [*disguised as* **Lucentio**],
Katherina, **Bianca**, [**Lucentio** *disguised as* **Cambio**,] *and*
others, [*along with*] *attendants*.

Baptista

appointed   [*to* **Tranio**] Signior Lucentio, this is the 'pointed° day
That Katherine and Petruchio should be married,
And yet we hear not of[1] our son-in-law.
What will be said? What mockery will it be

lack / is ready   To want° the bridegroom when the priest attends°   5
To speak the ceremonial rites of marriage?
What says Lucentio to this shame of ours?

Katherina

indeed   No shame but mine. I must, forsooth,° be forced
To give my hand, opposed against my heart,

ruffian / perversity   Unto a mad-brain rudesby,° full of spleen,°   10
Who wooed in haste and means to wed at leisure.

manic   I told you, I, he was a frantic° fool,

rude   Hiding his bitter jests in blunt° behavior,
And, to be noted for[2] a merry man,

appoint   He'll woo a thousand, 'point° the day of marriage,   15
Make feasts, invite friends, and proclaim the banns,[3]
Yet never means to wed where he hath wooed.
Now must the world point at poor Katherine
And say, "Lo, there is mad Petruchio's wife,
If it would please him come and marry her!"   20

Tranio

Patience, good Katherine, and Baptista too.
Upon my life, Petruchio means but well,
Whatever fortune stays him[4] from his word.
Though he be blunt, I know him passing wise;

nonetheless   Though he be merry, yet withal° he's honest.   25

1   *vex a very saint*

    Anger even a saint

2   *old*

    The addition of *old* **(absent from
    the Folio) seems demanded by
    Baptista's line that follows.** *Old* **here
    probably means "pleasurable,"
    though also carries with it the sense
    of "shabby," given the description
    of Petruchio in lines 41–60.**

3   *what to thine*

    What of your

Katherina

I wish Would° Katherine had never seen him, though!

She exits weeping [followed by Bianca and others].

Baptista

Go, girl. I cannot blame thee now to weep,

For such an injury would vex a very saint, [1]

Even / disposition Much° more a shrew of thy impatient humor.°

Enter **Biondello**.

Biondello

Master, master! News, and such old[2] news as you   30

never heard of!

Baptista

Is it new and old too? How may that be?

Biondello

Why, is it not news to hear of Petruchio's coming?

Baptista

Is he come?

Biondello

Why, no, sir.   35

Baptista

What then?

Biondello

He is coming.

Baptista

When will he be here?

Biondello

When he stands where I am and sees you there.

Tranio

But say, what to thine[3] old news?   40

1   *Why, Petruchio is coming*

See LONGER NOTE on page 296.

2   *thrice turned*

Turned inside out three times (to get more wear out of them)

3   *chapeless*

I.e., missing the *chape*, the metal tip that kept a sword from puncturing its sheath

4   *of no kindred*

Unmatched

5   *glanders*

A disease of horses similar to mumps

6   *like to mose in the chine*

This phrase is obscure; it seems to mean "likely to die (*mose* = mourn) of the disease (*glanders*)."

7   *lampass*

Swelling of the tissues in the mouth

8   *sped with spavins*

I.e., ruined with inflammation of the hocks (leg joints)

9   *rayed with the yellows*

Disfigured by jaundice

10   *the fives*

I.e., avives (an ear disease)

11   *stark spoiled with the staggers*

Totally ruined by staggering fits

12   *begnawn with the bots*

Infected with intestinal worms

13   *shoulder-shotten, near-legged before*

With dislocated shoulders and knock-kneed

14   *half-checked*

I.e., attached at one end only, meaning the horse could be turned in only one direction

15   *crupper*

Strap that runs around the horse's tail to secure the saddle

16   *kersey boot-hose*

Stockings of coarse woolen fabric, usually worn under riding boots

17   *and the humor of forty fancies pricked in 't*

With decoration that seems to be the product of forty different designers

Biondello

Why, Petruchio is coming[1] in a new hat and an old
jerkin,° a pair of old breeches thrice turned,[2] a pair of   *short coat*
boots that have been° candle cases, one buckled, an-   *i.e., been used for*
other laced; an old rusty sword ta'en out of the town
armory, with a broken hilt and chapeless,[3] with two   45
broken points; his horse hipped,° with an old mothy°   *lame / moth-eaten*
saddle and stirrups of no kindred,[4] besides possessed
with the glanders[5] and like to mose in the chine,[6]
troubled with the lampass,[7] infected with the farcins,°   *tumors*
full of windgalls,° sped with spavins,[8] rayed with the   50   *swollen hooves*
yellows,[9] past cure of the fives,[10] stark spoiled with the
staggers,[11] begnawn with the bots,[12] swayed in the back
and shoulder-shotten, near-legged before;[13] and with
a half-checked[14] bit and a headstall° of sheeps leather,   *i.e., halter*
which, being restrained° to keep him from stumbling,   55   *pulled*
hath been often burst° and now repaired with knots,   *broken*
one girth° six times pieced,° and a woman's crupper[15]   *saddle strap / repaired*
of velour,° which hath two letters° for her name fairly   *velvet / initials*
set down in studs, and here and there pieced with pack
thread.   60

Baptista

Who comes with him?

Biondello

Oh, sir, his lackey,° for all the world caparisoned° like the   *servant / dressed*
horse, with a linen stock° on one leg and a kersey boot-   *stocking*
hose[16] on the other, gartered with a red and blue list,° an   *strip of fabric*
old hat and the humor of forty fancies pricked in 't[17]   65
for° a feather. A monster, a very monster in apparel,   *instead of*
and not like a Christian footboy° or a gentleman's lackey.   *page*

Tranio

'Tis some odd humor° pricks° him to this fashion,   *mood / motivates*
Yet often times he goes but mean-appareled.°   *poorly dressed*

1   *all one*

The same thing

2   *by Saint Jamy*

A mild oath; *Saint Jamy* most likely
refers to the apostle James the
Greater, beheaded by Herod in A.D.
44. Sometime in the 9th century
the saint's bones were discovered
in Compostela in northwest Spain.
The shrine dedicated to the saint
became the most popular pilgrim-
age destination in Europe. The
jingle that line 77 introduces has
not been identified.

3   *come not well*

Petruchio puns on *welcome* in the
previous line and presumably
refers to the coldness he detects in
the greeting.

4   *yet you halt not*

(1) that doesn't seem to have
stopped you; (2) but you don't seem
to be limping (taking *come well* as
"walk normally"). In the following line, Tranio also puns on the
phrase, taking it now as "arrive well
dressed."

Baptista

I am glad he's come, howsoe'er he comes.   *70*

Biondello

Why, sir, he comes not.

Baptista

Didst thou not say he comes?

Biondello

Who? That Petruchio came?

Baptista

Ay, that Petruchio came.

Biondello

No, sir, I say his horse comes, with him on his back.   *75*

Baptista

Why, that's all one. [1]

Biondello

Nay, by Saint Jamy, [2]

bet   I hold° you a penny,

A horse and a man

Is more than one   *80*

And yet not many.

Enter **Petruchio** *and* **Grumio**.

Petruchio

gentlemen   Come, where be these gallants?° Who's at home?

Baptista

You are welcome, sir.

Petruchio

And yet I come not well. [3]

Baptista

And yet you halt not. [4]   *85*

Tranio

Not so well appareled as I wish you were.

1   *wherefore gaze this goodly company*

Why does everyone stare?

2   *wondrous monument*

Strange portent

3   *shame to your estate*

A disgrace to your social standing

4   *Though in some part enforcèd to digress*

**Though compelled to deviate
somewhat (from what I promised)**

5   *at more leisure*

When we have more time

Petruchio

Were it better I should rush in thus?

But where is Kate? Where is my lovely bride?

Gentlemen   How does my father? Gentles,° methinks you frown.

fine   And wherefore gaze this goodly° company [1]   90

As if they saw some wondrous monument, [2]

omen   Some comet or unusual prodigy? °

Baptista

Why, sir, you know this is your wedding day.

First were we sad, fearing you would not come,

unprepared   Now sadder that you come so unprovided. °   95

take off / outfit   Fie, doff ° this habit,° shame to your estate, [3]

An eyesore to our solemn festival.

Tranio

importance   And tell us what occasion of import°

Hath all so long detained you from your wife

And sent you hither so unlike yourself.   100

Petruchio

would be   Tedious it were° to tell and harsh to hear.

It suffices that   Sufficeth° I am come to keep my word,

Though in some part enforcèd to digress, [4]

explain   Which, at more leisure, [5] I will so excuse°

with   As you shall well be satisfied withal.°   105

But where is Kate? I stay too long from her.

slips away   The morning wears. ° 'Tis time we were at church.

Tranio

disgraceful   See not your bride in these unreverent° robes.

Go to my chamber; put on clothes of mine.

Petruchio

Not I, believe me. Thus I'll visit her.   110

Baptista

But thus, I trust, you will not marry her.

1   *Good sooth, even thus.*

    **I.e., In truth (I will), dressed just
    this way.**

2   *Could I repair what she will wear in me /
    As I can change these poor accoutrements*

    **If I could improve those aspects
    of me that she will experience as
    easily as I can change these shabby
    clothes (perhaps with a sexual in-
    nuendo, with *wear* = wear out)**

3   *to love concerneth us to add / Her father's
    liking*

    **I.e., it is crucial to add her father's
    approval to Bianca's love for you.**

4   *enjoy your hope*

    Get your wish

Petruchio

Good sooth, even thus.[1] Therefore, ha' done with
    words;

To me she's married, not unto my clothes.

Could I repair what she will wear in me

As I can change these poor accoutrements,[2]   115

'Twere well for Kate and better for myself.

But what a fool am I to chat with you,

morning   When I should bid good morrow° to my bride

contract / loving   And seal the title° with a lovely° kiss!

                           *He exits [with **Grumio**].*

Tranio

He hath some meaning in his mad attire.   120

We will persuade him, be it possible,

before   To put on better ere° he go to church.

Baptista

outcome   I'll after him, and see the event° of this.

     *He exits [with **Gremio**, **Biondello**, and attendants].*

Tranio

[to **Lucentio**] But sir, to love concerneth us to add

Her father's liking,[3] which to bring to pass,   125

disclosed   As before imparted° to your worship,

I am to get a man—whate'er he be

matters / purposes   It skills° not much; we'll fit him to our turn°—

And he shall be Vincentio of Pisa

guarantee   And make assurance° here in Padua   130

Of greater sums than I have promisèd.

So shall you quietly enjoy your hope[4]

And marry sweet Bianca with consent.

1   *steal our marriage*

     I.e., elope

2   *by degrees*

     Gradually

3   *watch our vantage*

     Look for opportunity

Lucentio

Were it not that my fellow schoolmaster

closely   Doth watch Bianca's steps so narrowly,°   135

'Twere good, methinks, to steal our marriage,[1]

i.e., even if   Which, once performed, let° all the world say no,

in spite   I'll keep mine own despite° of all the world.

Tranio

i.e., That possibility   That° by degrees[2] we mean to look into

And watch our vantage[3] in this business.   140

outwit   We'll overreach° the graybeard, Gremio,

nosy; suspicious   The narrow-prying° father, Minola,

clever   The quaint° musician, amorous Litio,

All for my master's sake, Lucentio.

Enter **Gremio**.

Signior Gremio, came you from the church?   145

Gremio

As willingly as e'er I came from school.

Tranio

And is the bride and bridegroom coming home?

Gremio

rude fellow   A bridegroom, say you? 'Tis a groom° indeed,

realize   A grumbling groom, and that the girl shall find.°

Tranio

more curst (quarrelsome)   Curster° than she? Why, 'tis impossible.   150

Gremio

Why, he's a devil, a devil, a very fiend.

Tranio

mother   Why, she's a devil, a devil, the devil's dam.°

Gremio

darling / compared to   Tut, she's a lamb, a dove, a fool° to° him!

I'll tell you, Sir Lucentio: when the priest

1   *Should ask*

     Asked

2   *by gogs wouns*

     **By God's wounds (a common oath
     that would be completely inappro-
     priate at a religious service)**

3   *took him such a cuff*

     Gave him such a smack

4   *for why*

     Because

5   *quaffed off the muscatel*

     **Drank up the *muscatel* (a sweet wine
     made from muscatel grapes)**

6   *sops*

     **Small cakes that were placed in the
     wine cups**

Should ask[1] if Katherine should be his wife,   155

"Ay, by gogs wouns!"[2] quoth he, and swore so loud

completely That, all° amazed, the priest let fall the book,

And, as he stooped again to take it up,

This mad-brained bridegroom took him such a cuff[3]

That down fell priest and book, and book and priest.   160

i.e., Petruchio / dare "Now take them up," quoth he,° "if any list."°

Tranio

i.e., the priest What said the wench when he° rose again?

Gremio

i.e., Petruchio Trembled and shook, for why[4] he° stamped and swore

cheat As if the vicar meant to cozen° him.

But, after many ceremonies done,   165

toast He calls for wine. "A health!"° quoth he, as if

on a ship He had been aboard,° carousing to his mates

After a storm; quaffed off the muscatel[5]

And threw the sops[6] all in the sexton's face,

Having no other reason   170

undernourished But that his beard grew thin and hungerly°

i.e., for the sops And seemed to ask him sops° as he was drinking.

This done, he took the bride about the neck

noisy And kissed her lips with such a clamorous° smack

That at the parting all the church did echo.   175

And I, seeing this, came thence for very shame,

crowd And after me, I know, the rout° is coming.

Such a mad marriage never was before.

Music plays.

Hark, hark! I hear the minstrels play.

Enter **Petruchio**, **Katherina**, **Bianca**,
Hortensio [*disguised as* **Litio**], **Baptista**,
[**Grumio**, *and others*].

1   *Make it no wonder.*

Don't be surprised.

Petruchio

trouble Gentlemen and friends, I thank you for your pains.° 180

expect I know you think° to dine with me today

amounts / refreshments And have prepared great store° of wedding cheer,°

But so it is my haste doth call me hence,

And therefore here I mean to take my leave.

Baptista

Is 't possible you will away tonight? 185

Petruchio

I must away today, before night come.

Make it no wonder.¹ If you knew my business,

You would entreat me rather go than stay.

worthy And, honest° company, I thank you all

That have beheld me give away myself 190

To this most patient, sweet, and virtuous wife.

toast Dine with my father, drink a health° to me,

For I must hence, and farewell to you all.

Tranio

Let us entreat you stay till after dinner.

Petruchio

It may not be.

Gremio

                    Let me entreat you. 195

Petruchio

It cannot be.

Katherina

                    Let me entreat you.

Petruchio

I am content.

Katherina

                    Are you content to stay?

Petruchio

I am content you shall entreat me stay,

1   *But yet not stay*

     But not content to stay

2   *The oats have eaten the horses.*

     **The comic inversion may be a com-
     ment either on the poor quality
     of the horse Petruchio has ridden
     (see lines 46–53) or on the general
     preposterousness of the situation.**

3   *jogging whiles your boots are green*

     **I.e., running off when your boots
     are new, a proverbial expression for
     "one who gets going early"**

4   *That take it on you at the first so roundly.*

     **I.e., when from the first you've been
     so eager to take charge**

5   *What hast thou to do?*

     What business is it of yours?

6   *stay my leisure*

     Wait until I am ready

7   *Carouse full measure to her maidenhead*

     Drink large toasts to her virginity.

But yet not stay, [1] entreat me how you can.

Katherina

Now, if you love me, stay.   200

Petruchio

Grumio, my horse.

Grumio

Ay, sir, they be ready. The oats have eaten the horses. [2]

Katherina

Nay, then,

Do what thou canst, I will not go today,

No, nor tomorrow, not till I please myself.   205

The door is open, sir. There lies your way.

You may be jogging whiles your boots are green. [3]

For me, I'll not be gone till I please myself.

extremely   'Tis like you'll prove a jolly° surly groom,

That take it on you at the first so roundly. [4]   210

Petruchio

i.e., I beg you   O Kate, content thee. Prithee,° be not angry.

Katherina

I will be angry. What hast thou to do? [5]

—Father, be quiet. He shall stay my leisure. [6]

Gremio

i.e., indeed   Ay, marry,° sir, now it begins to work.

Katherina

Gentlemen, forward to the bridal dinner.   215

I see a woman may be made a fool

If she had not a spirit to resist.

Petruchio

They shall go forward, Kate, at thy command.

—Obey the bride, you that attend on her.

enjoy yourselves   Go to the feast, revel and domineer,°   220

Carouse full measure to her maidenhead, [7]

exuberant   Be mad° and merry, or go hang yourselves.

1   *She is my goods, my chattels; she is my house, / My household stuff, my field, my barn, / My horse, my ox, my ass, my anything.*

While Petruchio sarcastically accuses the men of coveting Katherina, in fact, in the early modern period in which Shakespeare wrote, Petruchio's words would be almost literally true. Upon marriage, a woman's legal identity became subsumed by her husband's, a condition referred to as *coverture.* **Her right to execute legal arrangements could only be performed through her husband. All property that was not specifically reserved for the woman's use before marriage, as well as the woman's right to utilize such property, was transferred to her husband. In practice, however, women sometimes participated with their husbands in the financial management of the household. They often maintained control of their personal possessions and might be accorded "pin money" to use as they saw fit. Property that was reserved for them in the marriage arrangement would not be subject to their husbands' uses.**

2   *buckler*

Defend (a *buckler* **is a type of small shield)**

3   *a couple of quiet ones*

Said sarcastically

4   *Went they not*

If they had not left

5   *wants / For to supply*

Are not here to fill

6   *there wants no junkets*

There is no lack of delicacies.

As for But for° my bonny Kate, she must with me.

defiantly Nay, look not big,° nor stamp, nor stare, nor fret;

I will be master of what is mine own.   225

property She is my goods, my chattels;° she is my house,

My household stuff, my field, my barn,

My horse, my ox, my ass, my anything.[1]

And here she stands. Touch her whoever dare.

lawsuit/man I'll bring mine action° on the proudest he°   230

That stops my way in Padua.—Grumio,

surrounded Draw forth thy weapon; we are beset° with thieves.

Rescue thy mistress if thou be a man.

[*to* **Katherina**] Fear not, sweet wench; they shall not
          touch thee, Kate.

I'll buckler[2] thee against a million.   235

                    Petruchio, Katherina, [*and* **Grumio**] *exit.*

Baptista

Nay, let them go, a couple of quiet ones.[3]

Gremio

Went they not[4] quickly, I should die with laughing.

Tranio

Of all mad matches never was the like.

Lucentio

Mistress, what's your opinion of your sister?

Bianca

That being mad herself, she's madly mated.   240

Gremio

I warrant him, Petruchio is Kated.

Baptista

Neighbors and friends, though bride and bridegroom
          wants

For to supply[5] the places at the table,

You know there wants no junkets[6] at the feast.

1   *bride it*

Play the bride

[*to* **Tranio**] Lucentio, you shall supply the bridegroom's

place, 245

place And let Bianca take her sister's room.°

Tranio

Shall sweet Bianca practice how to bride it?¹

Baptista

She shall, Lucentio. Come, gentlemen; let's go.

They exit.

1   *a little pot and soon hot*

I.e., small and quick-tempered (a
proverbial expression)

2   *come by*

Find

3   *coldly*

(1) unenthusiastically; (2) affected
by the cold

4   *no greater a run*

No more of a running start

5   *fire, fire. Cast on no water.*

An allusion to a popular song
"Scotland's Burning," with a refrain, "Fire, fire! Fire, fire! / Cast on
water! Cast on water!"

Act 4, Scene 1

Enter **Grumio**.

Grumio

worthless horses Fie, fie on all tired jades,° on all mad masters, and all
roads foul ways!° Was ever man so beaten? Was ever man so
dirtied / ahead rayed?° Was ever man so weary? I am sent before° to
make a fire, and they are coming after to warm them.
Now, were not I a little pot and soon hot,[1] my very lips   5
might freeze to my teeth, my tongue to the roof of my
before mouth, my heart in my belly, ere° I should come by[2] a
fire to thaw me. But I with blowing the fire shall warm
myself. For, considering the weather, a taller man
catch than I will take° cold.—Holla, ho! Curtis!   10

Enter **Curtis**.

Curtis

Who is that calls so coldly?[3]

Grumio

A piece of ice. If thou doubt it, thou mayst slide from
my shoulder to my heel with no greater a run[4] but my
head and my neck. A fire, good Curtis.

Curtis

Is my master and his wife coming, Grumio?   15

Grumio

Oh, ay, Curtis, ay, and therefore fire, fire. Cast on no
water.[5]

Curtis

hot tempered Is she so hot° a shrew as she's reported?

Grumio

She was, good Curtis, before this frost. But thou
know'st winter tames man, woman, and beast,   20

1 *Why, thy horn is a foot, and so long am I,*
   at the least.

   The traditional symbol of a cuckold
   (a man whose wife had been un-
   faithful) was a *horn*; Grumio claims
   that Curtis has a cuckold's horn
   a foot long, and that he, Grumio,
   has a *horn* (penis) that is *at the least*
   that long.

2 *she being now at hand*

   Now that she is nearby

3 *hot office*

   Fire-making duties

4 *have thy duty*

   Take your payment

5 *Jack, boy! Ho, boy!*

   The first line of a popular song; the
   following line is, "News: the cat is
   in the well."

6 *cony-catching*

   Trickery (literally, *cony* means "rabbit"; here, *cony* refers to the victim
   of the deception). Curtis also puns
   on *catch*, a song or round, since
   Grumio is so obviously fond of such
   catches.

7 *Why, therefore fire, for I have caught*
   extreme cold.

   Grumio continues the word play,
   asking for *fire* to cook the *cony*, taking it in its original sense, and using
   caught, the past tense of "catch," to
   mean "be infected with."

8 *rushes strewed*

   Rushes were strewn on the floor as
   a sign of respect for special guests.

9 *fustian*

   Coarse cloth of blended cotton
   and flax

10 *Be the jacks fair within, the jills fair*
    without

    Jacks and *jills* refer to the male and
    female servants of the household,
    but also to types of drinking cups:
    jacks were leather cups that needed
    to be thoroughly scrubbed on the
    inside, while *jills* were a kind of
    small metal drinking cup, the out-
    side of which required polishing.

for it hath tamed my old master and my new mistress
and myself, fellow Curtis.

Curtis

i.e., tiny   Away, you three-inch° fool! I am no beast.

Grumio

Am I but three inches? Why, thy horn is a foot, and so
long am I, at the least.[1] But wilt thou make a fire, or   25

about   shall I complain on° thee to our mistress, whose hand,
she being now at hand,[2] thou shalt soon feel, to thy
cold comfort, for being slow in thy hot office?[3]

Curtis

I prithee, good Grumio, tell me how goes the world?

Grumio

duty   A cold world, Curtis, in every office° but thine, and   30
therefore fire! Do thy duty and have thy duty,[4] for my
master and mistress are almost frozen to death.

Curtis

There's fire ready, and therefore, good Grumio, the
news.

Grumio

Why, "Jack, boy! Ho, boy!"[5] and as much news as wilt   35
thou.

Curtis

Come, you are so full of cony-catching![6]

Grumio

Why, therefore fire, for I have caught extreme cold.[7]

tidied   Where's the cook? Is supper ready, the house trimmed,°
rushes strewed,[8] cobwebs swept, the servingmen in   40
their new fustian,[9] their white stockings, and every

servant   officer° his wedding garment on? Be the jacks fair

tablecloths   within, the jills fair without,[10] the carpets° laid, and
everything in order?

1   *fallen out*

    **Arguing (though playing on its
    literal sense in line 49)**

2   *thereby hangs a tale*

    **I.e., that reminds me of a story
    (proverbial)**

3   *sensible*

    **Both "making sense" and "able to
    be felt"**

4   *had'st thou not crossed*

    If you hadn't interrupted

Curtis

All ready. And therefore, I pray thee, news.   45

Grumio

First, know my horse is tired, my master and mistress
fallen out.[1]

Curtis

How?

Grumio

Out of their saddles into the dirt, and thereby hangs a
tale.[2]   50

Curtis

Let's ha' 't, good Grumio.

Grumio

Lend thine ear.

Curtis

Here.

Grumio

[*striking him*] There!

Curtis

This 'tis to feel a tale, not to hear a tale.   55

Grumio

And therefore 'tis called a sensible[3] tale. And this cuff° *blow*
was but to knock at your ear and beseech° listening. *request*
Now I begin: *Imprimis,*° we came down a foul° hill, my *First (Latin) / muddy*
master riding behind my mistress—

Curtis

Both of° one horse?   60 *on*

Grumio

What's that to thee?

Curtis

Why, a horse.

Grumio

Tell thou the tale! But had'st thou not crossed[4] me,

1   *with many things of worthy memory*

**Along with many other things
worth remembering**

2   *blue coats*

Blue **was the usual color for a servant's uniform.**

3   *horse-tail*

I.e., horse's tail

4   *kiss their hands*

**Kissing one's own hands was a
gesture of respect to a superior.**

5   *countenance*

**Pay respect to (as in line 89, but
Grumio in line 87 puns on it meaning "face")**

thou shouldst have heard how her horse fell, and she

muddy   under her horse. Thou shouldst have heard in how miry°   65

covered in dirt   a place, how she was bemoiled,° how he left her with

the horse upon her, how he beat me because her horse

stumbled, how she waded through the dirt to pluck

who   him off me, how he swore, how she prayed that° never

prayed before, how I cried, how the horses ran away,   70

broke / saddle strap   how her bridle was burst,° how I lost my crupper°—with

many things of worthy memory[1] which now shall die in

unenlightened   oblivion, and thou return unexperienced° to thy grave.

Curtis

account   By this reck'ning° he is more shrew than she.

Grumio

Ay, and that thou and the proudest of you all shall find   75

when he comes home. But what talk I of this? Call forth

Nathaniel, Joseph, Nicholas, Philip, Walter, Sugarsop,

and the rest. Let their heads be slickly combed, their

blue coats[2] brushed, and their garters of an indiffer-

matching   ent° knit. Let them curtsy with their left legs and not   80

presume to touch a hair of my master's horse-tail[3] till

they kiss their hands.[4] Are they all ready?

Curtis

They are.

Grumio

Call them forth.

Curtis

[*calling offstage*] Do you hear, ho? You must meet my   85

master to countenance[5] my mistress.

Grumio

Why? She hath a face of her own.

Curtis

Who knows not that?

1   *credit*

     Pay respect to (but in the following line, Grumio puns on *credit* in its financial sense)

2   *E'en at hand, alighted by this.*

     I.e., right here, dismounted by now.

Grumio

Thou, it seems, that calls for company to countenance
her.   90

Curtis

I call them forth to credit[1] her.

Grumio

Why, she comes to borrow nothing of them.

Enter four or five **Servingmen**.

Nathaniel

Welcome home, Grumio.

Philip

How now, Grumio?

Joseph

What, Grumio!   95

Nicholas

Fellow Grumio!

Nathaniel

How now, old lad?

Grumio

Welcome, you!—How now, you?—What, you!
—Fellow, you! And thus much for greeting. Now, my

dapper   spruce° companions, is all ready, and all things neat?   100

Nathaniel

All things is ready. How near is our master?

Grumio

E'en at hand, alighted by this.[2] And therefore be not—

i.e., God's   Cock's° passion, silence! I hear my master.

Enter **Petruchio** *and* [**Katherina**].

1   *hold my stirrup*

I.e., help me dismount

2   *malt-horse*

I.e., slow, stupid person. In breweries, the plodding *malt-horse* ground malt by walking in circles along a treadmill.

3   *park*

Enclosed hunting ground

4   *unpinked*

Undecorated (*pinked* shoes had small holes pierced in them, either as decoration or to attach ornamental beads and trim)

5   *link*

Torch (the burnt remains of which were used to blacken hats)

6   *sheathing*

I.e., having a sheath made or repaired

7   *Soud*

Unexplained; possibly the sound of humming or merely a misprint for "food"

Petruchio

Where be these knaves? What, no man at door
To hold my stirrup[1] nor to take my horse!   105
Where is Nathaniel, Gregory, Philip?

All Servingmen

Here! Here, sir! Here, sir!

Petruchio

"Here, sir! Here, sir! Here, sir! Here, sir!"

stupid   You loggerheaded° and unpolished grooms!
What, no attendance? No regard? No duty?   110
ahead   Where is the foolish knave I sent before?°

Grumio

previously   Here, sir, as foolish as I was before.°

Petruchio

bumpkin / i.e., worthless   You peasant swain!° You whoreson° malt-horse[2]
    drudge!
Did I not bid thee meet me in the park[3]
And bring along these rascal knaves with thee?   115

Grumio

Nathaniel's coat, sir, was not fully made,
shoes   And Gabriel's pumps° were all unpinked[4] i' th' heel.
There was no link[5] to color Peter's hat,
And Walter's dagger was not come from sheathing.[6]
ready   There were none fine° but Adam, Rafe, and Gregory.   120
The rest were ragged, old, and beggarly.
Yet, as they are, here are they come to meet you.

Petruchio

Go, rascals, go, and fetch my supper in.

                            Servingmen *exit.*

[*singing*]Where is the life that late I led?
Where are those—   125
Sit down, Kate, and welcome.
Soud,[7] soud, soud, soud!

1   *It was the friar of orders gray*

**The opening line of a bawdy song
about a nun's seduction by a Fran-
ciscan friar**

2   *mend the plucking off the other*

Take the other (boot) off properly.

3   *let it fall*

Spill it

4   *a fault unwilling*

I.e., an accident

5   *beetle-headed*

**Blockheaded (a *beetle* was a wooden
mallet)**

6   *give thanks*

Say grace

Enter **Servants** *with supper.*

Why, when, I say?—Nay, good sweet Kate, be merry.
—Off with my boots, you rogues! You villains, when?
　　[*sings*] It was the friar of orders gray, [1]　　　　130
　　As he forth walkèd on his way—
Stop / twist　—Out,° you rogue! You pluck° my foot awry.
Take that, and mend the plucking off the other. [2]
　　　　　　　　　　　　　　　　[*He kicks the servant.*]
Be merry, Kate.—Some water, here, what, ho!
Where's my spaniel Troilus? Sirrah, get you hence　　135
And bid my cousin Ferdinand come hither.
　　　　　　　　　　　　　　　　[*A servant exits.*]
One, Kate, that you must kiss and be acquainted with.
—Where are my slippers? Shall I have some water?

　　　　　Enter [*a servant*] *with water.*

Come, Kate, and wash, and welcome heartily.
—You whoreson villain! Will you let it fall? [3]　　　140
　　　　　　　　　　　　　　　　[*He strikes the servant.*]
Katherina
Patience, I pray you! 'Twas a fault unwilling. [4]
Petruchio
A whoreson, beetle-headed, [5] flap-eared knave!
appetite　—Come, Kate, sit down. I know you have a stomach.°
Will you give thanks, [6] sweet Kate, or else shall I?
—What's this? Mutton?
First Servant
　　　　　　　　Ay.
Petruchio
　　　　　　　　　　Who brought it?
Peter
　　　　　　　　　　　　　　I.　　145

1   *dresser*

    Sideboard or serving table

2   *I'll be with you straight.*

    I'll deal with you right away.

3   *if you were so contented*

    I.e., if you had seen fit (to eat it)

4   *choler*

    **Anger; hot headedness. According
    to Elizabethan physiology, *choler*
    was caused by an excess of yellow
    bile, one of the four *humors* (bodily
    fluids) that determined a person's
    mood, health, and personality.
    Choler was associated with heat
    and dryness, therefore *burnt and
    dried* up meat was to be avoided.**

5   *Since of ourselves, ourselves are choleric*

    **I.e., since we're both naturally
    choleric**

6   *for company*

    Together

7   *He kills her in her own humor.*

    **He subdues her by behaving exactly
    as she does.**

Petruchio

'Tis burnt, and so is all the meat.

What dogs are these! Where is the rascal cook?

dared   How durst° you, villains, bring it from the dresser [1]

And serve it thus to me that love it not?

wooden plates   There, take it to you—trenchers,° cups, and all!   150

[**Petruchio** *throws the food and dishes at the servants.*]

blockheads   You heedless joltheads° and unmannered slaves!

What, do you grumble? I'll be with you straight. [2]

[*Servants exit.*]

Katherina

upset   I pray you, husband, be not so disquiet.°

The meat was well, if you were so contented. [3]

Petruchio

up   I tell thee, Kate, 'twas burnt and dried away,°   155

And I expressly am forbid to touch it,

For it engenders choler, [4] planteth anger,

And better 'twere that both of us did fast,

Since of ourselves, ourselves are choleric, [5]

Than feed it with such over-roasted flesh.   160

Be patient. Tomorrow 't shall be mended,

And, for this night, we'll fast for company. [6]

Come; I will bring thee to thy bridal chamber.

They exit.

separately   Enter **Servants** *severally.* °

Nathaniel

Peter, didst ever see the like?

Peter

He kills her in her own humor. [7]   165

1   *making a sermon of continency*

Delivering a lecture on self-control

2   *Thus have I politicly begun my reign*

In what follows, Petruchio com-
pares his taming of Katherina to
the training of a hawk or falcon.
The metaphor connects to other
images in the play describing Katherina as a wild creature. But equally
important, it marks Petruchio's
claim to be a gentleman and hence
perhaps to his insistence on taming rather than physical coercion.
According to George Turberville's
*The Book of Falconry or Hawking; For the
Only Delight and Pleasure of All Noble-
men and Gentlemen* (1575), falconry
was a sport of wellborn men and
designed not to break the spirit of
the bird but to train it. Later, at the
start of the contest in Act Five, after
Katherina has been "tamed," Petruchio distinguishes her from his
animals when he says that he will
wager twenty crowns on his "hawk
or hound," but "twenty times so
much" on his wife (5.2.74–75).

3   *passing empty*

With a completely empty stomach

4   *stoop*

Submit; also with the technical
sense in falconry of "fly to the
falconer (or the prey)"

5   *never looks upon her lure*

Never obeys the falconer's command (the *lure* was the device used
to recall the falcon)

6   *man my haggard*

Tame my hawk (a *haggard* was an
untamed female hawk)

7   *watch her*

Keep her from sleeping

8   *kites*

A type of hawk, with a possible pun
on "Kate"

9   *bate and beat*

Flutter and flap (their wings)

Enter **Curtis**, *a servant.*

Grumio

Where is he?

Curtis

In her chamber, making a sermon of continency[1]
to her,

scolds And rails and swears and rates,° that she, poor soul,

Knows not which way to stand, to look, to speak,   170

And sits as one new-risen from a dream.

Away, away, for he is coming hither!   [*They exit.*]

Enter **Petruchio**.

Petruchio

shrewdly Thus have I politicly° begun my reign,[2]

And 'tis my hope to end successfully.

hungry My falcon now is sharp° and passing empty,[3]   175

fed adequately And, till she stoop,[4] she must not be full-gorged,°

For then she never looks upon her lure.[5]

Another way I have to man my haggard,[6]

To make her come and know her keeper's call:

That is, to watch her,[7] as we watch these kites[8]   180

That bate and beat[9] and will not be obedient.

She ate no meat today, nor none shall eat.

Last night she slept not, nor tonight she shall not.

As with the meat, some undeservèd fault

I'll find about the making of the bed,   185

And here I'll fling the pillow, there the bolster,

blanket This way the coverlet,° another way the sheets.

chaos / pretend Ay, and amid this hurly° I intend°

respectful That all is done in reverend° care of her.

1   *'tis charity to show*

**It would be a good deed to show me
(a way to tame her better).**

stay awake   And, in conclusion, she shall watch° all night,   190
And if she chance to nod I'll rail and brawl,
And with the clamor keep her still awake.
This is a way to kill a wife with kindness,
disposition   And thus I'll curb her mad and headstrong humor.°
He that knows better how to tame a shrew,   195
Now let him speak; 'tis charity to show.¹   *He exits.*

1   *bears me fair in hand*

     Gives me strong encouragement

2   *resolve me that*

     Answer that for me

3   The Art to Love

     Ovid's poem on erotic love and
     seduction is normally known in
     English as *The Art of Love (Ars Amato-*
     ria). **See 3.1.28–29 and note.**

4   *proceeders*

     I.e., those who proceed to the next
     stage (an academic term for those
     who advance from one academic
     degree to the next)

Act 4, Scene 2

Enter **Tranio** [*disguised as* **Lucentio**] *and* **Hortensio**
[*disguised as* **Litio**].

Tranio

Is 't possible, friend Litio, that mistress Bianca

love   Doth fancy° any other but Lucentio?

I tell you, sir, she bears me fair in hand. [1]

Hortensio

convince   Sir, to satisfy° you in what I have said,

Stand by and mark the manner of his teaching.   5

[*They move aside.*]

Enter **Bianca** [*and* **Lucentio** *disguised as* **Cambio**].

Lucentio

Now, mistress, profit you in what you read?

Bianca

What, master, read you? First resolve me that. [2]

Lucentio

that which / practice   I read that° I profess,° *The Art to Love.* [3]

Bianca

And may you prove, sir, master of your art.

Lucentio

While you, sweet dear, prove mistress of my heart!   10

[*They move aside.*]

Hortensio

i.e., indeed   [*coming forward*] Quick proceeders, [4] marry!° Now, tell
    me, I pray,

dared   You that durst° swear that your mistress Bianca

Loved none in the world so well as Lucentio.

Tranio

O despiteful love! Unconstant womankind!

astonishing   I tell thee, Litio, this is wonderful!°   15

1   *cullion*

    **Despicable fellow (literally,
    "testicle")**

2   *entire affection*

    Total devotion

3   *Would all the world but he had quite
    forsworn!*

    **I wish everyone in the world besides
    Cambio would swear similarly (i.e.,
    to abandon Bianca).**

4   *In resolution*

    Determined

Hortensio

Mistake no more. I am not Litio,

Nor a musician as I seem to be,

disdains   But one that scorn° to live in this disguise

For such a one as leaves a gentleman

And makes a god of such a cullion.¹   20

Know, sir, that I am called Hortensio.

Tranio

Signior Hortensio, I have often heard

Of your entire affection² to Bianca,

inconstancy   And since mine eyes are witness of her lightness, °

I will with you, if you be so contented,   25

i.e., swear to abandon   Forswear° Bianca and her love forever.

Hortensio

See how they kiss and court! Signior Lucentio,

Here is my hand, and here I firmly vow

Never to woo her more, but do forswear her

of all   As one unworthy all° the former favors   30

foolishly / with   That I have fondly° flattered her withal. °

Tranio

sincere   And here I take the like unfeignèd° oath

beg   Never to marry with her, though she would entreat. °

indecently   Fie on her! See how beastly° she doth court him!

Hortensio

Would all the world but he had quite forsworn!³   35

For me, that I may surely keep mine oath,

I will be married to a wealthy widow

Before / who   Ere° three days pass, which° hath as long loved me

untamed female hawk   As I have loved this proud disdainful haggard. °

And so farewell, Signior Lucentio.   40

Kindness in women, not their beauteous looks,

Shall win my love, and so I take my leave,

In resolution⁴ as I swore before.   *[He exits.]*

1   *case*

Circumstance (though *case* could
also mean (1) disguise; (2) vagina)

2   *forsworn you*

Sworn to give you up

3   *tricks eleven and twenty long*

I.e., exactly how (from the card
game *one-and-thirty*, in which the
object is to end with a score of
precisely *eleven and twenty*; see 1.2.31
and note)

4   *charm*

I.e., quiet with a magic spell

Tranio

[*moving forward*] Mistress Bianca, bless you with such
    grace

belongs   As 'longeth° to a lover's blessèd case!¹   45

i.e., off guard   Nay, I have ta'en you napping,° gentle love,

And have forsworn you² with Hortensio.

Bianca

Tranio, you jest. But have you both forsworn me?

Tranio

Mistress, we have.

Lucentio

                  Then we are rid of Litio.

Tranio

I' faith, he'll have a lusty widow now   50

That shall be wooed and wedded in a day.

Bianca

God give him joy!

Tranio

Ay, and he'll tame her.

Bianca

He says so, Tranio?

Tranio

Faith, he is gone unto the taming school.   55

Bianca

The taming school? What? Is there such a place?

Tranio

Ay, mistress, and Petruchio is the master,

That teacheth tricks eleven and twenty long³

To tame a shrew and charm⁴ her chattering tongue.

      Enter **Biondello**.

Biondello

O master, master, I have watched so long   60

1   *ancient angel*

I.e., worthy old fellow (with a pun
on *angel*, the gold coin stamped
with the image of the archangel
Michael; also, possibly "guardian
angel")

2   *formal in apparel*

Dressed formally

3   *gait and countenance*

Walk and appearance

4   *let me alone*

Let me handle things.

5   **Merchant**

The Folio reads *Pedant* here and in
all subsequent stage directions and
speech prefixes, perhaps because
as the text was copied the scribe
took the unfamiliar *marcantant* in
line 64 as a synonym for "pedant."
Whatever the case, it seems clear
that the character is, as in the
sources, a merchant; see, for
example, the itinerary in lines
75–77, as well as lines 90–91 and 111,
and 4.4.24–25. This edition emends
accordingly.

6   *at the farthest*

At your destination

That I am dog-weary, but at last I spied

An ancient angel [1] coming down the hill

i.e., purpose   Will serve the turn.°

Tranio

                What is he, Biondello?

Biondello

merchant/schoolteacher   Master, a marcantant° or a pedant,°

I know not what, but formal in apparel, [2]   65

In gait and countenance [3] surely like a father.

Lucentio

And what of him, Tranio?

Tranio

gullible   If he be credulous° and trust my tale,

pretend to be   I'll make him glad to seem° Vincentio

And give assurance to Baptista Minola   70

As if he were the right Vincentio.

Take in your love and then let me alone. [4]

                [**Lucentio** *and* **Bianca** *exit.*]

Enter a [**Merchant**].[5]

Merchant

God save you, sir.

Tranio

            And you, sir. You are welcome.

further   Travel you far° on, or are you at the farthest? [6]

Merchant

Sir, at the farthest for a week or two,   75

But then up farther, and as far as Rome,

And so to Tripoli, if God lend me life.

Tranio

What countryman, I pray?

Merchant

                Of Mantua.

1   *goes hard*

     Is serious

2   *but that you are but newly come*

     **Except for the fact that you've only
     just arrived**

3   *else proclaimed about*

     Announced in various places

4   *bills for money by exchange*

     **Promissory notes that can be
     exchanged for money (much like
     modern traveler's checks)**

5   *sooth to say*

     Truth be told

Tranio

Of Mantua, sir? Marry, God forbid!

And come to Padua, careless of your life?   80

Merchant

My life, Sir? How, I pray? For that goes hard.[1]

Tranio

'Tis death for anyone in Mantua

To come to Padua. Know you not the cause?

i.e., Mantuan / detained   Your° ships are stayed° at Venice, and the Duke,

Because of a   For° private quarrel 'twixt your Duke and him,   85

Hath published and proclaimed it openly.

i.e., surprising   'Tis marvel,° but that you are but newly come,[2]

You might have heard it else proclaimed about.[3]

Merchant

that   Alas, sir, it is worse for me than so,°

For I have bills for money by exchange[4]   90

From Florence and must here deliver them.

Tranio

Well, sir, to do you courtesy,

This will I do, and this I will advise you.

First tell me, have you ever been at Pisa?

Merchant

Ay, sir, in Pisa have I often been,   95

respectable   Pisa renownèd for grave° citizens.

Tranio

Among them know you one Vincentio?

Merchant

I know him not, but I have heard of him:

A merchant of incomparable wealth.

Tranio

He is my father, sir, and sooth to say,[5]   100

appearance   In count'nance° somewhat doth resemble you.

1   *and all one*

    **But what difference does that
    make?**

2   *Look that you take upon you as you
    should.*

    **I.e., see that you act the part
    appropriately.**

3   *make the matter good*

    Carry out the plan

4   *let you understand*

    Will explain to you

5   *looked for*

    Expected

6   *pass assurance of a dower*

    **Guarantee the financial arrange-
    ments (see 2.1.120–124 and note)**

7   *becomes you*

    Is appropriate for your role

Biondello

[*aside*] As much as an apple doth an oyster, and all one.[1]

Tranio

dire circumstance To save your life in this extremity,°

This favor will I do you for his sake,

And think it not the worst of all your fortunes 105

That you are like to Sir Vincentio:

reputation / assume His name and credit° shall you undertake,°

hospitably And in my house you shall be friendly° lodged.

Look that you take upon you as you should.[2]

In this way You understand me, sir? So° shall you stay 110

Till you have done your business in the city.

If this be court'sy, sir, accept of it.

Merchant

consider O sir, I do, and will repute° you ever

The patron of my life and liberty.

Tranio

Then go with me to make the matter good.[3] 115

This, by the way, I let you understand:[4]

My father is here looked for[5] every day

To pass assurance of a dower[6] in marriage

Between 'Twixt° me and one Baptista's daughter here.

In all these circumstances I'll instruct you. 120

Go with me to clothe you as becomes you.[7]   *They exit.*

1   *The more my wrong, the more his spite*

     appears.

     The more I suffer, the greater is his anger toward me.

2   *Upon entreaty have a present alms*

     Upon asking immediately receive charity

3   *never needed that I should entreat*

     Never needed to beg

Act 4, Scene 3

Enter **Katherina** *and* **Grumio**.

Grumio

honestly   No, no, forsooth.° I dare not for my life.

Katherina

The more my wrong, the more his spite appears. [1]

What, did he marry me to famish me?

Beggars that come unto my father's door

Upon entreaty have a present alms. [2]   5

If not, elsewhere they meet with charity.

But I, who never knew how to entreat,

Nor never needed that I should entreat, [3]

food   Am starved for meat,° giddy for lack of sleep,

swearing   With oaths° kept waking and with brawling fed;   10

vexes / things I lack   And that which spites° me more than all these wants, °

He does it under name of perfect love,

As who should say, if I should sleep or eat,

'Twere deadly sickness or else present death.

food   I prithee go and get me some repast.°   15

I care not what, so it be wholesome food.

Grumio

ox's   What say you to a neat's° foot?

Katherina

surpassingly   'Tis passing° good. I prithee let me have it.

Grumio

anger inducing   I fear it is too choleric° a meat.

cow's stomach   How say you to a fat tripe° finely broiled?   20

Katherina

I like it well. Good Grumio, fetch it me.

Grumio

I cannot tell. I fear 'tis choleric.

What say you to a piece of beef and mustard?

1   *let the mustard rest*

     Forget the mustard

2   *the very name*

     Only the name

3   *Sorrow on*

     May sorrow fall on

4   *what cheer*

     **How are your spirits (but Katherina
     takes it to mean "how has your
     reception been?")**

Katherina

A dish that I do love to feed upon.

Grumio

Ay, but the mustard is too hot a little.   25

Katherina

Why, then the beef, and let the mustard rest. [1]

Grumio

Nay then, I will not. You shall have the mustard,

Or else you get no beef of Grumio.

Katherina

Then both, or one, or anything thou wilt.

Grumio

Why, then the mustard without the beef.   30

Katherina

lying   Go; get thee gone, thou false deluding° slave,

                                          Beats him.

That feed'st me with the very name [2] of meat.

Sorrow on [3] thee and all the pack of you

gloat   That triumph° thus upon my misery.

Go; get thee gone, I say.   35

        Enter **Petruchio** *and* **Hortensio**, *[and a servant]*
        with meat.

Petruchio

darling / dejected   How fares my Kate? What, sweeting,° all amort?°

Hortensio

Mistress, what cheer? [4]

Katherina

                    Faith, as cold as can be.

Petruchio

Pluck up thy spirits. Look cheerfully upon me.

Here love, thou see'st how diligent I am,

prepare   To dress° thy meat myself and bring it thee.   40

1   *all my pains is sorted to no proof*

      **All my efforts have gone for
      nothing.**

2   *revel it as bravely*

      Celebrate as finely dressed

3   *ruffs*

      **Large circular collars of pleated
      fabric**

4   *farthingales*

      Petticoats with large hoops

5   *double change of brav'ry*

      Two changes of fine clothing

I am sure, sweet Kate, this kindness merits thanks.
What, not a word? Nay, then thou lov'st it not,
And all my pains is sorted to no proof. [1]
[to servant] Here, take away this dish.

Katherina

                               I pray you, let it stand.

Petruchio

The poorest service is repaid with thanks,   45
And so shall mine before you touch the meat.

Katherina

I thank you, sir.

Hortensio

Signior Petruchio, fie, you are to blame.
Come, mistress Kate; I'll bear you company.

Petruchio

[aside to **Hortensio**] Eat it up all, Hortensio, if thou
    lovest me.   50
—Much good do it unto thy gentle heart.

quickly   Kate, eat apace;° and now, my honey love,
Will we return unto thy father's house
And revel it as bravely[2] as the best,
With silken coats and caps and golden rings,   55
With ruffs[3] and cuffs and farthingales[4] and things,
With scarves and fans and double change of brav'ry,[5]
decadent stuff   With amber bracelets, beads, and all this knav'ry.°
awaits   What, hast thou dined? The tailor stays° thy leisure
frilly   To deck thy body with his ruffling° treasure.   60

*Enter **Tailor**.*

Come, tailor, let us see these ornaments.
Lay forth the gown.

1   *doth fit the time*

Is the latest fashion

2   *in haste*

Soon

3   *me say*

My speaking

4   *best you*

You should

Enter **Haberdasher.**

                              What news with you, sir?
    Haberdasher
order Here is the cap your Worship did bespeak. °
    Petruchio
porridge bowl Why, this was molded on a porringer! °
vulgar / disgusting A velvet dish! Fie, fie, 'tis lewd ° and filthy! °   65
cockleshell Why, 'tis a cockle ° or a walnut shell,
knickknack / trifle A knack, ° a toy, a trick, ° a baby's cap.
  Away with it! Come, let me have a bigger.
    Katherina
  I'll have no bigger. This doth fit the time, [1]
  And gentlewomen wear such caps as these.   70
    Petruchio
calm; mild When you are gentle, ° you shall have one too,
  And not till then.
    Hortensio
                [*aside*] That will not be in haste. [2]
    Katherina
permission Why, sir, I trust I may have leave ° to speak,
  And speak I will. I am no child, no babe.
  Your betters have endured me say [3] my mind,   75
  And if you cannot, best you [4] stop your ears.
  My tongue will tell the anger of my heart,
  Or else my heart, concealing it, will break;
  And, rather than it shall, I will be free
  Even to the uttermost, as I please, in words.   80
    Petruchio
  Why, thou say'st true. It is a paltry cap,
pastry shell / trifle A custard-coffin, ° a bauble, ° a silken pie.
  I love thee well in that thou lik'st it not.

1   *masquing stuff*

Fancy costume (masques were
elaborate dramatic productions
often performed at court)

2   *censer*

Incense holder (usually with ornate
perforations); it isn't clear what the
reference to *a barber's shop* implies,
except as a place where scissors and
knives were used.

3   *mar it to the time*

Ruin it forever

4   *hop me over every kennel home*

I.e., hop home over every open
sewer (*me* is a colloquialism calling
attention to the speaker, here
meaning something like "as far as I
am concerned")

Katherina

Love me or love me not, I like the cap,

And it I will have, or I will have none. 85

Petruchio

Thy gown? Why, ay. Come, tailor, let us see 't.

[**Haberdasher** *exits.*]

O mercy, God! What masquing stuff[1] is here?

small cannon What's this? A sleeve? 'Tis like a demi-cannon. °

What, up and down, carved like an apple tart?

Here's snip and nip and cut and slish and slash, 90

Like to a censer[2] in a barber's shop.

i.e., in the Why, what a'° devil's name, tailor, call'st thou this?

Hortensio

[*aside*] I see she's like to have neither cap nor gown.

Tailor

asked You bid° me make it orderly and well,

According to the fashion and the time. 95

Petruchio

i.e., Indeed Marry,° and did. But if you be remembered,

I did not bid you mar it to the time. [3]

Go; hop me over every kennel home, [4]

business For you shall hop without my custom,° sir.

Leave I'll none of it. Hence;° make your best of it. 100

Katherina

I never saw a better-fashioned gown,

skillfully made More quaint,° more pleasing, nor more commendable.

Perhaps / plaything Belike° you mean to make a puppet° of me.

Petruchio

Why, true, he means to make a puppet of thee.

Tailor

She says your Worship means to make a puppet of her. 105

1   *Thou liest, thou thread, thou thimble, /*
     Thou yard, three-quarters, half-yard,
     quarter, nail!

     No doubt because of their asso-
     ciation with women and women's
     clothes, tailors were proverbially
     effeminate. Here Petruchio asserts
     his own masculinity by mocking
     the tailor's small size, but espe-
     cially the inadequacy of his rapidly
     shrinking "yard" (or "yardstick"),
     a slang word for "penis." A *nail* was
     one-sixteenth of a yard.

2   *Braved*

     Defied, but punning on the sense
     of "dressed up" or "decked out,"
     as one might expect from a tailor;
     Grumio puns similarly in line 123.

3   *bemete*

     Thoroughly measure (i.e., wallop)

Petruchio

O monstrous arrogance! Thou liest, thou thread, thou
    thimble,

i.e., quarter yard   Thou yard, three-quarters, half-yard, quarter,° nail!¹

louse egg   Thou flea, thou nit,° thou winter cricket thou!

spool   Braved² in mine own house with a skein° of thread?

fragment   Away, thou rag, thou quantity,° thou remnant,   110

i.e., yardstick   Or I shall so bemete³ thee with thy yard°

your chattering   As thou shalt think on prating° whilst thou liv'st!

I tell thee, I, that thou hast marred her gown.

Tailor

Your Worship is deceived. The gown is made

Just as my master had direction.   115

Grumio gave order how it should be done.

Grumio

material   I gave him no order. I gave him the stuff.°

Tailor

But how did you desire it should be made?

Grumio

Marry, sir, with needle and thread.

Tailor

But did you not request to have it cut?   120

Grumio

decorated   Thou hast faced° many things.

Tailor

I have.

Grumio

Defy   Face° not me. Thou hast braved many men; brave not

me. I will neither be faced nor braved. I say unto thee, I

bid thy master cut out the gown, but I did not bid him   125

Therefore (Latin)   cut it to pieces. *Ergo,*° thou liest.

1   *note of the fashion*

    Order for the gown

2   *in 's throat*

    Outrageously

3   *bill*

    **I.e., the *note*, or order, for the gown
    mentioned in line 127.**

4   *prove upon thee*

    Establish by fighting you

Tailor

Why, here is the note of the fashion [1] to testify.

[*holding up a paper*]

Petruchio

Read it.

Grumio

it The note lies in 's throat, [2] if he° say I said so.

Tailor

First (Latin) [*reads*] "Imprimis,° a loose-bodied gown—"   130

Grumio

Master, if ever I said "loose-bodied gown," sew me in

spool the skirts of it, and beat me to death with a bottom°

of brown thread. I said "a gown."

Petruchio

[*to* **Tailor**] Proceed.

Tailor

small semicircular [*reads*] "With a small-compassed° cape—"   135

Grumio

I confess the cape.

Tailor

wide [*reads*] "With a trunk° sleeve—"

Grumio

I confess two sleeves.

Tailor

intricately [*reads*] "The sleeves curiously° cut."

Petruchio

Ay, there's the villany.   140

Grumio

Error i' th' bill, [3] sir; error i' th' bill! I commanded the

sleeves should be cut out and sewed up again, and that

I'll prove upon thee, [4] though thy little finger be armed

in a thimble.

1   *in place where*

In a suitable place (presumably a court of law rather than the place for fighting that Grumio seeks)

2   *I am for thee straight.*

I am ready to fight you now.

3   *God-a-mercy*

God have mercy (an exclamation like "for God's sake")

4   *take it up unto thy master's use*

I.e., take it away and let your master find some other

5   *Take up*

I.e., lift up; Grumio pretends to understand Petruchio as saying that he wants the tailor's master to lift up Katherina's dress in order to have sex with her.

6   *deeper than you think for*

More serious than you imagine, with a pun on *deeper* in a sexual sense.

7   *Commend me*

Give my regards

8   *honest mean habiliments*

Respectable humble clothes

Tailor

if This is true that I say; an° I had thee in place where, [1]   145
thou shouldst know it.

Grumio

I am for thee straight.[2] Take thou the bill, give me thy

yardstick mete-yard,° and spare not me.

Hortensio

chance God-a-mercy,[3] Grumio! Then he shall have no odds.°

Petruchio

[*to* **Tailor**] Well, sir, in brief, the gown is not for me.   150

Grumio

You are i' th' right, sir, 'tis for my mistress.

Petruchio

Go; take it up unto thy master's use.[4]

Grumio

Villain, not for thy life! Take up[5] my mistress' gown
for thy master's use?

Petruchio

meaning Why, sir, what's your conceit° in that?   155

Grumio

Oh, sir, the conceit is deeper than you think for.[6] Take up
my mistress' gown to his master's use! Oh, fie, fie, fie!

Petruchio

[*aside*] Hortensio, say thou wilt see the tailor paid.

away [*to* **Tailor**] Go, take it hence.° Begone, and say no more.

Hortensio

[*aside to* **Tailor**] Tailor, I'll pay thee for thy gown tomorrow.   160

brusque Take no unkindness of his hasty° words.

Away, I say. Commend me[7] to thy master.

Tailor *exits.*

Petruchio

i.e., will go Well, come, my Kate. We will° unto your father's
Even in these honest mean habiliments.[8]

1   *lay it on*

    Blame

2   *hence forthwith*

    Leave immediately

3   *sport us*

    Celebrate

4   *ere I go to horse*

    Before I mount my horse

5   *still crossing*

    Always contradicting

full	Our purses shall be proud,° our garments poor, 165
	For 'tis the mind that makes the body rich;
	And, as the sun breaks through the darkest clouds,
through / clothing	So honor peereth in° the meanest habit.°
	What, is the jay more precious than the lark
	Because his feathers are more beautiful? 170
	Or is the adder better than the eel
patterned	Because his painted° skin contents the eye?
	Oh, no, good Kate. Neither art thou the worse
clothing / accessories	For this poor furniture° and mean array.°
	If thou account'st it shame, lay it on¹ me, 175
celebrate	And therefore frolic!° We will hence forthwith²
	To feast and sport us³ at thy father's house.
	[*to* **Grumio**] Go call my men, and let us straight to him,
	And bring our horses unto Long Lane end.
	There will we mount, and thither walk on foot. 180
	Let's see, I think 'tis now some seven o'clock,
i.e., lunchtime	And well we may come there by dinnertime.°

Katherina

I dare assure you, sir, 'tis almost two,

the evening meal And 'twill be supper° time ere you come there.

Petruchio

It shall be seven ere I go to horse.⁴   185

whatever Look, what° I speak, or do, or think to do,
You are still crossing⁵ it.—Sirs, let 't alone.
I will not go today, and ere I do
It shall be what o'clock I say it is.

Hortensio

[*aside*] Why, so this gallant will command the sun.   190

[*They exit.*]

1   booted and bareheaded

**In the Folio, this appears as part
of an erroneous repetition of the
entry of the Merchant after line 18.**

2   *Please it you that*

Would you like it if

3   *but I be*

Unless I am

4   *hold your own*

Stay in your role

5   *looked for*

Expected

Act 4, Scene 4

*Enter **Tranio** [disguised as **Lucentio**] and the **Merchant**,
booted and bareheaded*[1] *[and] dressed like **Vincentio**.*

Tranio

Sir, this is the house. Please it you that[2] I call?

Merchant

Ay, what else? And but I be[3] deceived,

Signior Baptista may remember me

Nearly — Near° twenty years ago, in Genoa,

(the name of an inn) Where we were lodgers at the Pegasus.°   5

Tranio

'Tis well; and hold your own,[4] in any case,

gravity / belongs With such austerity° as 'longeth° to a father.

Merchant

promise I warrant° you.

*Enter **Biondello**.*

But, sir, here comes your boy.

given his instructions 'Twere good he were schooled.°

Tranio

Fear you not him.—Sirrah Biondello,   10

thoroughly Now do your duty throughly,° I advise you.

real Imagine 'twere the right° Vincentio.

Biondello

Tut, fear not me.

Tranio

But hast thou done thy errand to Baptista?

Biondello

I told him that your father was at Venice,   15

And that you looked for[5] him this day in Padua.

1   *Hold thee that to drink.*

   Take that (coin) and buy yourself a drink.

2   *Set your countenance*

   Put on the appropriate expression.

3   *stand*

   Prove yourself a

4   *gather in*

   Collect

5   *With one consent*

   I.e., to join with you

Tranio

worthy   Thou'rt a tall° fellow. Hold thee that to drink.[1]

                                       [*gives him money*]

         Enter **Baptista** *and* **Lucentio** [*disguised*
         as **Cambio**].

Here comes Baptista. Set your countenance,[2] sir.

—Signior Baptista, you are happily met.

[*to the* **Merchant**] Sir, this is the gentleman I told you of.   20

I pray you stand[3] good father to me now:

Give me Bianca for my patrimony.

Merchant

Quiet   Soft,° son.

[*to* **Baptista**] Sir, by your leave, having come to Padua

To gather in[4] some debts, my son Lucentio   25

matter   Made me acquainted with a weighty cause°

Of love between your daughter and himself.

because of   And, for° the good report I hear of you

And for the love he beareth to your daughter

delay   And she to him, to stay° him not too long,   30

I am content, in a good father's care,

married   To have him matched.° And if you please to like

No worse than I, upon some agreement

Me shall you find ready and willing

With one consent[5] to have her so bestowed,   35

too demanding   For curious° I cannot be with you,

Signior Baptista, of whom I hear so well.

Baptista

Sir, pardon me in what I have to say.

brevity   Your plainness and your shortness° please me well.

Right true it is your son Lucentio here   40

Doth love my daughter, and she loveth him,

1   *such assurance ta'en / As shall with either part's agreement stand*

The contracts drawn up that we would each find acceptable

2   *Pitchers have ears*

Proverbial for "someone might overhear us." (A pitcher's handle was called an *ear*.)

3   *heark'ning still*

Always listening

4   *an it like you*

If it please you

5   *slender warning*

Short notice

6   *a thin and slender pittance*

A skimpy meal

pretend	Or both dissemble° deeply their affections.
	And therefore, if you say no more than this,
	That like a father you will deal with him
offer/dowry	And pass° my daughter a sufficient dower,° 45
	The match is made, and all is done:
	Your son shall have my daughter with consent.

Tranio

I thank you, sir. Where then do you know best

engaged   We be affied° and such assurance ta'en

And shall with either part's agreement stand? [1]   50

Baptista

Not in my house, Lucentio, for you know

Pitchers have ears, [2] and I have many servants.

Besides, old Gremio is heark'ning still, [3]

perhaps   And happily° we might be interrupted.

Tranio

Then at my lodging, an it like you. [4]   55

lodge   There doth my father lie,° and there this night

conduct   We'll pass° the business privately and well.

i.e., Lucentio   Send for your daughter by your servant° here.

i.e., Biondello/notary   My boy° shall fetch the scrivener° presently.

The worst is this: that at so slender warning [5]   60

likely   You are like° to have a thin and slender pittance. [6]

Baptista

pleases/hurry   It likes° me well.—Cambio, hie° you home

herself   And bid Bianca make her° ready straight.

And, if you will, tell what hath happenèd:

Lucentio's father is arrived in Padua,   65

likely   And how she's like° to be Lucentio's wife.

                           [**Lucentio** *exits.*]

Biondello

I pray the gods she may, with all my heart!

1   *Dally not with*

     Don't joke about

2   *get thee gone*

     The Folio follows this with a stage
     direction, *Enter Peter*. As the charac-
     ter has nothing to say and plays no
     apparent role in the action here, it
     seems likely that this entrance is
     accidently left over from something
     that was eventually cut.

3   Enter **Lucentio** [disguised as
     Cambio] and **Biondello**.

     Technically, as the stage has been
     emptied and new characters enter,
     a new scene should begin here (as
     it does in a number of 18th-century
     editions). Possibly Biondello only
     moves away and greets Lucentio as
     he enters.

Tranio

Dally not with ¹ the gods, but get thee gone.²

—Signior Baptista, shall I lead the way?

[**Biondello**] *exits.*

dish / entertainment   Welcome! One mess° is like to be your cheer.°   70

improve   Come, sir; we will better° it in Pisa.

Baptista

I follow you.   [**Tranio, Merchant,** *and* **Baptista**] *exit.*

Enter **Lucentio** [*disguised as* **Cambio**] *and*
Biondello.³

Biondello

Cambio.

Lucentio

What say'st thou, Biondello?

Biondello

at   You saw my master wink and laugh upon° you?   75

Lucentio

Biondello, what of that?

Biondello

Faith, nothing, but he's left me here behind to ex-

interpret / signals   pound° the meaning or moral of his signs and tokens.°

Lucentio

explain   I pray thee, moralize° them.

Biondello

Then thus: Baptista is safe, talking with the deceiving   80
father of a deceitful son.

Lucentio

And what of him?

Biondello

His daughter is to be brought by you to the supper.

Lucentio

And then?

1   *counterfeit assurance*

     Fraudulent contract

2   *Take your assurance of her*

     Make your claim to her legal

3   cum privilegio ad imprimendum
     solum

     "With the sole right to print"
     (Latin), a familiar formula used to
     indicate a publisher's monopoly,
     used here to express the husband's
     parallel monopoly of his wife for
     the fathering of a child.

4   *as she went to the garden for parsley to*
     stuff a rabbit

     I.e., when she least expected it

5   *against you come with your appendix*

     In preparation for your arrival with
     your appendage (i.e., Bianca).
     Biondello continues the printing
     metaphor by comparing Bianca,
     who will come after Lucentio, to an
     ***appendix* that is added at the end of**
     a book.

6   *Hap what hap may*

     Whatever happens

7   *roundly go about her*

     Boldly pursue her

8   *It shall go hard*

     I.e., it would be a pity

Biondello

The old priest at Saint Luke's Church is at your com-   85
mand at all hours.

Lucentio

And what of all this?

Biondello

I cannot tell, except they are busied about a counterfeit assurance.[1] Take your assurance of her[2] *cum privile-*
gio ad imprimendum solum.[3] To th' church take the priest,   90
clerk, and some sufficient honest witnesses.

what   If this be not that° you look for, I have no more to say,
But bid Bianca farewell forever and a day.

Lucentio

Hear'st thou, Biondello—

Biondello

wait   I cannot tarry.° I knew a wench married in an afternoon   95
as she went to the garden for parsley to stuff a rabbit,[4]
and so may you, sir. And so adieu, sir. My master hath
assigned   appointed° me to go to Saint Luke's to bid the priest be
ready to come against you come with your appendix.[5]

He exits.

Lucentio

I may, and will, if she be so contented.   100
why   She will be pleased. Then wherefore° should I doubt?
Hap what hap may,[6] I'll roundly go about her.[7]
It shall go hard[8] if "Cambio" go without her.   *He exits.*

1   *Or ere*

     I.e., before

2   *Evermore crossed*

     Always contradicted

3   *An if*

     If

4   *rush candle*

     **Improvised candle made from
     grease and a reed (*rush*) for a wick**

Act 4, Scene 5

Enter **Petruchio**, **Katherina**, **Hortensio**, [*and servants*].

Petruchio

i.e., in / i.e., Baptista's Come on, a° God's name, once more toward our father's.°

splendidly Good Lord, how bright and goodly° shines the moon!

Katherina

The moon? The sun! It is not moonlight now.

Petruchio

I say it is the moon that shines so bright.

Katherina

I know it is the sun that shines so bright. 5

Petruchio

Now, by my mother's son, and that's myself,

please It shall be moon, or star, or what I list,°

Or ere¹ I journey to your father's house.

[*to the servants*] Go on, and fetch our horses back again.

[*Servants exit.*]

—Evermore crossed² and crossed, nothing but

crossed! 10

Hortensio

[*to* **Katherina**] Say as he says, or we shall never go.

Katherina

Forward, I pray, since we have come so far,

And be it moon, or sun, or what you please.

An if³ you please to call it a rush candle,⁴

Henceforth I vow it shall be so for me. 15

Petruchio

I say it is the moon.

Katherina

I know it is the moon.

Petruchio

Nay, then you lie. It is the blessèd sun.

1   *even as*

Just like

2   *go thy ways*

Do what you please.

3   *Thus the bowl should run, / And not unluckily against the bias*

I.e., now we are on the proper course. In the game of *bowls*, the ball swerves because of a weight (*bias*) placed on one side. Petruchio claims that his relationship with Katherina now follows her natural inclination rather than runs *against* it.

4   *Whither away*

Where are you going?

5   *favorable stars*

Good fortune

Katherina

Then, God be blessed, it is the blessèd sun.

But sun it is not, when you say it is not,   20

And the moon changes even as [1] your mind.

What you will have it named, even that it is,

And so it shall be so for Katherine.

Hortensio

battlefield   Petruchio, go thy ways; [2] the field° is won.

Petruchio

Well, forward, forward! Thus the bowl should run,   25

And not unluckily against the bias. [3]

But, soft! Company is coming here.

Enter **Vincentio**.

[*to* **Vincentio**] Good morrow, gentle mistress, where

    away?

—Tell me, sweet Kate, and tell me truly too,

lovelier   Hast thou beheld a fresher° gentlewoman?   30

Such war of white and red within her cheeks!

adorn   What stars do spangle° Heaven with such beauty

suit; look well in   As those two eyes become° that heavenly face?

[*to* **Vincentio**] Fair lovely maid, once more good day to

    thee.

—Sweet Kate, embrace her for her beauty's sake.   35

Hortensio

He   [*aside*] A'° will make the man mad, to make the woman

of him.

Katherina

Young budding virgin, fair and fresh and sweet,

home   Whither away, [4] or where is thy abode?°

Happy the parents of so fair a child.   40

to whom   Happier the man whom° favorable stars [5]

1   *reverend father*

Respectable old man

2   *loving father*

Petruchio expands the meaning of
***father* from "old man" (as it is in line**
49) to his brother-in-law's father (a
kind of extended father-in-law), as
Vincentio's son, Lucentio, will be
married to Bianca—though Petru-
chio cannot know this information
at this point in the play. (See line 76
and note.)

Give Allots° thee for his lovely bedfellow!
Petruchio
insane Why, how now, Kate! I hope thou art not mad.°
This is a man—old, wrinkled, faded, withered—
And not a maiden, as thou say'st he is. 45
Katherina
Pardon, old father, my mistaking eyes
That have been so bedazzled with the sun
young That everything I look on seemeth green.°
Now I perceive thou art a reverend father.[1]
Pardon, I pray thee, for my mad mistaking. 50
Petruchio
also Do, good old grandsire, and withal° make known
Which way thou travellest. If along with us,
for We shall be joyful of° thy company.
Vincentio
Fair sir, and you, my merry mistress,
greeting That with your strange encounter° much amazed me, 55
My name is called Vincentio, my dwelling Pisa,
And bound I am to Padua, there to visit
who A son of mine which° long I have not seen.
Petruchio
What is his name?
Vincentio
Lucentio, gentle sir. 60
Petruchio
Fortunately Happily° met, the happier for thy son.
And now, by law as well as reverend age,
I may entitle thee my loving father.[2]
The sister to my wife, this gentlewoman,
this time Thy son by this° hath married. Wonder not 65
reputation Nor be not grieved. She is of good esteem,°
Her dowry wealthy, and of worthy birth;

1   *so qualified*

Having such qualities

2   *break a jest*

Play a joke

3   *so it is*

It is so (though neither Hortensio
nor Petruchio can know this, for
the wedding has not yet taken
place and neither has any reason to
think it will. Shakespeare seems to
be compressing the action of the
play to bring it more swiftly to a
conclusion.)

4   *put me in heart*

Encouraged me

5   *Have to*

I.e., Now I am ready to go after

suit Beside, so qualified [1] as may beseem°

   The spouse of any noble gentleman.

   Let me embrace with old Vincentio,   70

   And wander we to see thy honest son,

at Who will of° thy arrival be full joyous.

   Vincentio

   But is this true, or is it else your pleasure,

   Like pleasant travelers, to break a jest [2]

pass Upon the company you overtake?°   75

   Hortensio

   I do assure thee, father, so it is. [3]

   Petruchio

of this Come; go along and see the truth hereof, °

joke/suspicious For our first merriment° hath made thee jealous. °

         [*All except* **Hortensio**] *exit.*

   Hortensio

   Well, Petruchio, this has put me in heart. [4]

unreasonable Have to [5] my widow, and if she be froward,°   80

stubborn Then hast thou taught Hortensio to be untoward.°

                 He exits.

1   is out before

     Has already entered alone

2   *I fly*

     I'm off

3   *the church a' your back*

     I.e., I'll see you married.

4   *You shall not choose but*

     You must

5   *command your welcome*

     Order some hospitality for you

6   *some cheer is toward*

     **Some refreshment is being
     prepared.**

7   *You were best*

     You had better

8   [**Merchant**] looks out of the
     window.

     **In Elizabethan outdoor theaters
     such as the Theatre or the Globe,
     the Merchant would likely have
     appeared in the small gallery that
     overlooked the stage (see Fig. 1 on
     page 306). This gallery was used for
     such staging purposes and, later,
     for musicians; rich theatergoers
     sometimes paid extra to be seated
     here, often, thus, called "the Lords'
     room."**

Act 5, Scene 1

Enter **Biondello**, **Lucentio**, *and* **Bianca**. **Gremio** *is out before.* [1]

Biondello

Quietly   Softly° and swiftly, sir, for the priest is ready.

Lucentio

happen   I fly, [2] Biondello. But they may chance° to need thee at
home; therefore leave us.

[**Lucentio** *and* **Bianca**] *exit.*

Biondello

Nay, faith, I'll see the church a' your back, [3] and then
come back to my master's as soon as I can.   [*He exits.*]   5

Gremio

wonder why / time   I marvel° Cambio comes not all this while.°

Enter **Petruchio**, [**Katherina**], **Vincentio**,
Grumio, *with attendants.*

Petruchio

Sir, here's the door. This is Lucentio's house.

i.e., Baptista's / lies   My father's° bears° more toward the marketplace.

To there   Thither° must I, and here I leave you, sir.

Vincentio

You shall not choose but [4] drink before you go.   10
I think I shall command your welcome [5] here,
And, by all likelihood, some cheer is toward. [6]

Knock[s].

Gremio

They're busy within. You were best [7] knock louder.

[**Merchant**] *looks out of the window.* [8]

1   *pound*

The basic monetary unit of
16th-century England. See Induction, scene 1, line 17 and note.

2   *make merry*

Celebrate

3   *frivolous circumstances*

Meaningless details

4   *to Padua*

The Folio prints "from Padua" here,
which seems clearly an error, as
they are in Padua. Emending the
preposition seems the simplest
correction, though many editions
have changed the place name to
Pisa or Mantua.

5   *flat knavery*

Outright villainy

6   *under my countenance*

Using my identity

Merchant

Who's / as if What's° he that knocks as° he would beat down the
    gate?

Vincentio

Is Signior Lucentio within, sir?   15

Merchant

with He's within, sir, but not to be spoken withal.°

Vincentio

What if a man bring him a hundred pound[1] or two to
make merry[2] withal?

Merchant

Keep your hundred pounds to yourself. He shall need
none so long as I live.   20

Petruchio

Nay, I told you your son was well beloved in Padua.
[*to* **Merchant**] Do you hear, sir? To leave frivolous
circumstances,[3] I pray you tell Signior Lucentio that
his father is come to Padua[4] and is here at the door to
speak with him.   25

Merchant

Thou liest. His father is come from Padua and here
looking out at the window.

Vincentio

Art thou his father?

Merchant

Ay, sir, so his mother says, if I may believe her.

Petruchio

[*to* **Vincentio**] Why, how now, gentleman! Why, this is   30
flat knavery[5] to take upon you another man's name.

Merchant

he / cheat Lay hands on the villain. I believe 'a° means to cozen°
somebody in this city under my countenance.[6]

Enter **Biondello**.

1   *good shipping*

    Good sailing (i.e., good luck)

2   *crack-hemp*

    **Rogue; villain (i.e., someone likely
    to strain or *crack* a hangman's *hemp*
    rope)**

3   *I hope I may choose*

    I hope I have a choice

Biondello

[*aside*] I have seen them in the church together. God
send 'em good shipping! [1] But who is here? Mine old   35
master Vincentio! Now we are undone and brought to
nothing.

Vincentio

[*to* **Biondello**] Come hither, crack-hemp. [2]

Biondello

I hope I may choose, [3] sir.

Vincentio

Come hither, you rogue! What, have you forgot me?   40

Biondello

Forgot you! No, sir. I could not forget you, for I never
saw you before in all my life.

Vincentio

What? You notorious villain, didst thou never see thy
master's father, Vincentio?

Biondello

i.e., indeed What, my old worshipful old master? Yes, marry,° sir.   45
See where he looks out of the window.

Vincentio

Is 't so, indeed.   *He beats* **Biondello**.

Biondello

Help, help, help! Here's a madman will murder me.

[*He exits.*]

Merchant

Help, son! Help, Signior Baptista!

[*He exits from above.*]

Petruchio

Prithee, Kate, let's stand aside and see the end of this   50
controversy.   [*They move aside.*]

Enter [**Merchant**] *with servants,* **Baptista**, [*and*]
Tranio [*disguised as* **Lucentio**].

1   *play the good husband*

     Act like a careful financial manager

2   *Bergamo*

     **Bergamo , an inland city, about
     twenty-five miles northeast of
     Milan, was notorious for rude
     speech.**

Tranio

presume   Sir, what are you that offer° to beat my servant?

Vincentio

What am I, sir? Nay, what are you, sir? O immortal
well-dressed / short jacket gods! O fine° villain! A silken doublet,° a velvet hose,
high-crowned   a scarlet cloak, and a copatain° hat! Oh, I am undone; I   55
am undone! While I play the good husband[1] at home,
my son and my servant spend all at the university.

Tranio

How now, what's the matter?

Baptista

What, is the man lunatic?

Tranio

clothes   Sir, you seem a sober ancient gentleman by your habit,°   60
but your words show you a madman. Why, sir, what
concerns   'cerns° it you if I wear pearl and gold? I thank my good
afford   father I am able to maintain° it.

Vincentio

Thy father? O villain! He is a sailmaker in Bergamo.[2]

Baptista

You mistake, sir; you mistake, sir. Pray, what do you   65
think is his name?

Vincentio

His name? As if I knew not his name! I have brought
him up ever since he was three years old, and his
name is Tranio.

Merchant

Away, away, mad ass! His name is Lucentio, and he   70
is mine only son and heir to the lands of me, Signior
Vincentio.

Vincentio

Lucentio? Oh, he hath murdered his master! —Lay hold

1   *Lay hold on*

     Seize

2   *forthcoming*

     I.e., ready to stand trial

3   *wert best*

     Had better

on[1] him. I charge you in the Duke's name.—O my son,
my son!—Tell me, thou villain, where is my son Lucentio?   75
Tranio
Call forth an officer.   [*An attendant exits.*]

[*Enter an officer.*]

Father-in-law Carry this mad knave to the jail.—Father° Baptista,
I charge you see that he be forthcoming.[2]
Vincentio
Carry me to the jail?
Gremio
Wait Stay,° officer. He shall not go to prison.   80
Baptista
Talk not, Signior Gremio. I say he shall go to prison.
Gremio
tricked Take heed, Signior Baptista, lest you be cony-catched°
in this business. I dare swear this is the right Vincentio.
Merchant
Swear if thou dar'st.
Gremio
Nay, I dare not swear it.   85
Tranio
Then thou wert best[3] say that I am not Lucentio.
Gremio
Yes, I know thee to be Signior Lucentio.
Baptista
old fool Away with the dotard!° To the jail with him!
Vincentio
harassed Thus strangers may be haled° and abused.—O
monstrous villain!   90

Enter **Biondello**, **Lucentio**, *and* **Bianca**.

1   *While counterfeit supposes bleared*
     thine eyne
     While false impressions blurred
     your sight (*eyne* is an archaic plural
     of "eyes")

2   *with a witness*
     Beyond doubt

3   *faced and braved*
     Confronted and defied

4   *Cambio is changed*
     In Italian, *cambio* means "change."

5   *bear my countenance*
     Assume my identity

6   *at the last*
     Finally

Biondello

ruined Oh, we are spoiled,° and yonder he is! Deny him,
forswear him, or else we are all undone.

> **Biondello, Tranio,** *and* [**Merchant**]
> *exit* [*with officer*], *as fast as may be.*

Lucentio

(*kneel*[*s*]) Pardon, sweet father.

Vincentio

Lives my sweet son?

Bianca

[*kneels*] Pardon, dear father.   95

Baptista

How hast thou offended? Where is Lucentio?

Lucentio

Here's Lucentio, right son to the right Vincentio,
That have by marriage made thy daughter mine
While counterfeit supposes bleared thine eyne.¹

Gremio

plotting Here's packing,° with a witness,² to deceive us all!   100

Vincentio

Where is that damnèd villain, Tranio,
That faced and braved³ me in this matter so?

Baptista

Why, tell me, is not this my Cambio?

Bianca

Cambio is changed⁴ into Lucentio.

Lucentio

Love wrought these miracles. Bianca's love   105
position Made me exchange my state° with Tranio,
While he did bear my countenance⁵ in the town,
And happily I have arrived at the last⁶
Unto the wishèd haven of my bliss.

1   *good will*

     Consent

2   *Go to.*

     **An exclamation of impatience
(here, "Relax!")**

3   *sound the depth of this knavery*

     To see how far this villainy goes

4   *My cake is dough*

     I.e., my plans are ruined

5   *Out of hope of all*

     With no hope for anything

What Tranio did, myself enforced him to.   110
Then pardon him, sweet father, for my sake.

Vincentio

I'll slit the villain's nose that would have sent me to the jail.

Baptista

But do you hear, sir? Have you married my daughter
without asking my good will? [1]

Vincentio

satisfy Fear not, Baptista; we will content° you. Go to.[2] But I   115
go in   will in° to be revenged for this villainy.   *He exits.*

Baptista

And I, to sound the depth of this knavery.[3]   *He exits.*

Lucentio

Look not pale, Bianca. Thy father will not frown.

[**Lucentio** *and* **Bianca**] *exit.*

Gremio

My cake is dough,[4] but I'll in among the rest,
Out of hope of all[5] but my share of the feast.   [*He exits.*]   120

Katherina

fuss   Husband, let's follow to see the end of this ado.°

Petruchio

First kiss me, Kate, and we will.

Katherina

What, in the midst of the street?

Petruchio

What, art thou ashamed of me?

Katherina

No, sir, God forbid, but ashamed to kiss.   125

Petruchio

Why, then let's home again. [*to* **Grumio**] Come, sirrah,
let's away.

1   *Better once than never, for never too late.*

Petruchio combines two proverbs:
"Better late than never" and "It is
never too late to mend."

Katherina

Nay, I will give thee a kiss. [*They kiss.*] Now pray thee,
  love, stay.

Petruchio

Is not this well? Come, my sweet Kate.

i.e., sometime Better once° than never, for never too late.[1]   *They exit.*

1   *close our stomachs up*

    (1) round off our meal; (2) end any quarrels

2   *great good cheer*

    Fine wedding celebration

3   *kind*

    (1) affectionate; (2) natural

4   *Then never trust me if I be afeard.*

    The Widow takes Petruchio's *fears* to mean "frightens."

Act 5, Scene 2

Enter **Baptista**, **Vincentio**, **Gremio**, *the* [**Merchant**],
Lucentio, **Bianca**, [**Petruchio**, **Katherina**, **Hortensio**,]
Tranio, **Biondello**, **Grumio**, *and* **Widow**, *the*

i.e., dessert *Servingmen with Tranio bringing in a banquet.* °

Lucentio

long delayed At last, though long, ° our jarring notes agree,
And time it is when raging war is done
escapes / avoided To smile at 'scapes° and perils overblown. °
My fair Bianca, bid my father welcome,
While I with selfsame kindness welcome thine.   5
Brother Petruchio, sister Katherina,
And thou, Hortensio, with thy loving widow,
Feast with the best, and welcome to my house.
My banquet is to close our stomachs up,[1]
After our great good cheer.[2] Pray you, sit down,   10
For now we sit to chat as well as eat.

Petruchio

Nothing but sit and sit, and eat and eat!

Baptista

provides Padua affords° this kindness, son Petruchio.

Petruchio

Padua affords nothing but what is kind.[3]

Hortensio

For both our sakes, I would that word were true.   15

Petruchio

Now, for my life, Hortensio fears his widow.

Widow

Then never trust me if I be afeard.[4]

Petruchio

You are very sensible, and yet you miss my sense:
I mean, Hortensio is afeard of you.

1   *Thus I conceive by him.*

     i.e., That's what I think about him
     (but Petruchio pretends to take
     ***conceive* to mean "get pregnant").**

2   *conceives her tale*

     i.e., intends her statement (with
     an unwitting pun on "tail," a slang
     term for "genitals")

3   *mean indeed, respecting you*

     (1) quite moderate compared to
     you; (2) just as nasty dealing with
     you

4   *A hundred marks*

     I.e., I'll bet a hundred marks. A
     ***mark* was worth $^2/_3$ of a pound; as**
     a laborer might make only five or
     six pounds a year, this was a very
     large bet.

5   *does put her down*

     Defeats her (but Hortensio takes it
     in a bawdy sense)

Widow

dizzy He that is giddy° thinks the world turns round.   20

Petruchio

Boldly Roundly° replied.

Katherina

Mistress, how mean you that?

Widow

Thus I conceive by him. [1]

Petruchio

Conceives by me? How likes Hortensio that?

Hortensio

My widow says, thus she conceives her tale. [2]   25

Petruchio

Very well mended. Kiss him for that, good widow.

Katherina

"He that is giddy thinks the world turns round"—
I pray you, tell me what you meant by that.

Widow

Your husband being troubled with a shrew

his own (Petruchio's) Measures my husband's sorrow by his° woe.   30
And now you know my meaning.

Katherina

nasty A very mean° meaning.

Widow

                      Right, I mean you.

Katherina

And I am mean indeed, respecting you. [3]

Petruchio

Go after To° her, Kate!

Hortensio

To her, widow!   35

Petruchio

A hundred marks [4] my Kate does put her down. [5]

1   *officer*

    **Petruchio picks up Hortensio's
    word, *office*, and suggests that
    Hortensio is ready to fulfill his
    marital obligations (i.e., have sex).**

2   *head and horn*

    **I.e., the *head* you *butt* with has horns
    (implying Gremio is a cuckold)**

3   *Have at you*

    I.e., be prepared

4   *shift my bush*

    **I.e., hide somewhere else (with
    a possible pun on *bush* meaning
    "pubic hair")**

Hortensio

job   That's my office.°

Petruchio

i.e., Here's   Spoke like an officer![1] Ha'° to thee, lad!

>   [*He*] *drinks to* **Hortensio**.

Baptista

How likes Gremio these quick-witted folks?

Gremio

butt heads   Believe me, sir, they butt° together well.   40

Bianca

quick-witted   Head and butt! An hasty-witted° body

Would say your head and butt were head and horn.[2]

Vincentio

Ay, mistress bride, hath that awakened you?

Bianca

frightened   Ay, but not frighted° me. Therefore I'll sleep again.

Petruchio

Nay, that you shall not. Since you have begun,   45

sarcastic   Have at you[3] for a bitter° jest or two!

Bianca

prey; target   Am I your bird?° I mean to shift my bush,[4]

And then pursue me as you draw your bow.

—You are welcome all.

>   **Bianca** [, **Katherina**, *and* **Widow**] *exit.*

Petruchio

stopped   She hath prevented° me. Here, Signior Tranio,   50

This bird you aimed at, though you hit her not;

toast   Therefore a health° to all that shot and missed.

Tranio

unleashed   Oh, sir, Lucentio slipped° me like his greyhound,

Which runs himself and catches for his master.

1   *something currish*

Somewhat mean-spirited (*currish* meaning "like a snarling mongrel dog" rather than like a well-bred *greyhound*)

2   *hold you at a bay*

Keeps you at a distance; holds you off

3   *good sadness*

All seriousness

4   *for assurance*

As a test; the Folio reads "sir assurance," and it is tempting to read this as a personification of overconfidence (i.e., "Sir Assurance") if it were not that both Hortensio and Lucentio are addressed and that "for" and "sir" are easily confused in manuscript.

5   *crowns*

Gold coins

Petruchio

A good swift simile, but something currish. [1]   55

Tranio

'Tis well, sir, that you hunted for yourself.

'Tis thought your deer does hold you at a bay. [2]

Baptista

Oh, oh, Petruchio! Tranio hits you now.

Lucentio

taunt I thank thee for that gird,° good Tranio.

Hortensio

Confess, confess; hath he not hit you here?   60

Petruchio

He/scratched A'° has a little galled° me, I confess,

bounce And, as the jest did glance° away from me,

wounded 'Tis ten to one it maimed° you two outright.

Baptista

Now, in good sadness, [3] son Petruchio,

greatest I think thou hast the veriest° shrew of all.   65

Petruchio

Well, I say no; and therefore, for assurance, [4]

Let's each one send unto his wife,

And he whose wife is most obedient

To come at first when he doth send for her

Shall win the wager which we will propose.   70

Hortensio

Content. What's the wager?

Lucentio

Twenty crowns. [5]

Petruchio

Twenty crowns?

wager/on I'll venture° so much of° my hawk or hound,

But twenty times so much upon my wife.   75

Lucentio

A hundred then.

1   *A match!*

Agreed

2   *be your half*

Put up half your wager

Hortensio

Content.

Petruchio

A match!¹ 'Tis done.

Hortensio

Who shall begin?

Lucentio

That will I.   80

Go, Biondello; bid your mistress come to me.

Biondello

I go.   *He exits.*

Baptista

Son, I'll be your half² Bianca comes.

Lucentio

I'll have no halves. I'll bear it all myself.

Enter **Biondello**.

How now, what news?   85

Biondello

Sir, my mistress sends you word

That she is busy, and she cannot come.

Petruchio

Really   How!° "She's busy, and she cannot come!"

Is that an answer?

Gremio

                    Ay, and a kind one too.

Pray God, sir, your wife send you not a worse.   90

Petruchio

i.e., for a better one   I hope better.°

Hortensio

request   Sirrah Biondello, go and entreat° my wife

immediately   To come to me forthwith.°

                              Biondello *exits.*

1   *must needs*
    Will have to

2   *goodly jest*
    Excellent joke

3   *The fouler fortune mine*
    Then I will have the worse luck.

4   *by my holidam*
    An oath, meaning "by everything I hold sacred."

Petruchio
Oh, ho, entreat her!
Nay, then she must needs[1] come.   95
Hortensio
I am afraid, sir,
Do what you can, yours will not be entreated.

Enter **Biondello**.

Now, where's my wife?
Biondello
She says you have some goodly jest[2] in hand.
She will not come. She bids you come to her.   100
Petruchio
Worse and worse. She will not come?
O vile, intolerable, not to be endured!
—Sirrah Grumio, go to your mistress,
Say I command her come to me.

[**Grumio**] *exits.*

Hortensio
I know her answer.   105
Petruchio
What?
Hortensio
She will not.
Petruchio
i.e., end to the matter The fouler fortune mine,[3] and there an end.°

Enter **Katherina**.

Baptista
Now, by my holidam,[4] here comes Katherina!

1   *Swinge me them*

    **Beat them (*me* is a colloquialism
    calling attention to the speaker,
    here meaning "for me")**

2   *awful*

    Inspiring awe; worthy of respect

3   *what not*

    Everything

4   *as she had never been*

    **I.e., as if what she previously was
    had never existed**

Katherina

What is your will, sir, that you send for me?   110

Petruchio

Where is your sister and Hortensio's wife?

Katherina

They sit conferring by the parlor fire.

Petruchio

refuse   Go fetch them hither. If they deny° to come,

Swinge me them [1] soundly forth unto their husbands.

immediately   Away, I say, and bring them hither straight.°   115

[**Katherina** *exits.*]

Lucentio

miracle   Here is a wonder,° if you talk of a wonder.

Hortensio

portends   And so it is. I wonder what it bodes.°

Petruchio

Marry, peace it bodes, and love, and quiet life,

proper   An awful [2] rule, and right° supremacy,

And, to be short, what not [3] that's sweet and happy.   120

Baptista

good fortune   Now, fair° befall thee, good Petruchio!

The wager thou hast won, and I will add

Unto their losses twenty thousand crowns,

Another dowry to another daughter,

For she is changed as she had never been. [4]   125

Petruchio

Nay, I will win my wager better yet,

And show more sign of her obedience,

Her new-built virtue and obedience.

Enter [**Katherina**], **Bianca** *and* **Widow**.

1 *brought to such a silly pass*

I.e., made to behave so ridiculously

2 *Fie, fie! Unknit that threat'ning unkind brow*

Katherina's speech ignores the traditional biblical justification for women's inferiority as punishment for Eve's transgression in Eden that predominated in texts about appropriate roles for women. Instead, it appeals to a more secular argument grounded in nature and the difference between the sexes: the distinction between women's "soft and weak and smooth bodies" and those bodies that men commit "to painful labor" for women's "maintenance." Also, as Lynda E. Boose points out (see For Further Reading), Katherina's final gesture of placing her hand beneath Petruchio's foot in "token" of her "duty" replicates one of the rituals of the wedding ceremony that women were often required to perform in pre-Reformation England and Europe. That Shakespeare resurrects this ceremony may suggest how thoroughly implicated in dominant, male-centered ideologies Katherina's speech is. Conversely, it does not seem too far-fetched to imagine that Shakespeare may be subtly undercutting the ideas in Katherina's speech by introducing onstage a ritual form thoroughly antiquated by the early 1590s. In any case, it is worth noting that this is the longest speech in the play, which perhaps itself is enough to suggest that there is something more complex than mere submission implied.

3 *Confounds thy fame*

Ruins your reputation

stubborn See where she comes and brings your froward° wives
As prisoners to her womanly persuasion. 130
—Katherine, that cap of yours becomes you not.
trifle Off with that bauble;° throw it underfoot.

[*She drops her cap.*]

Widow

Lord, let me never have a cause to sigh,
Till I be brought to such a silly pass! [1]

Bianca

Fie! What a foolish duty call you this? 135

Lucentio

I would your duty were as foolish too.
The wisdom of your duty, fair Bianca,
Hath cost me one hundred crowns since suppertime.

Bianca

betting The more fool you for laying° on my duty.

Petruchio

Katherine, I charge thee, tell these headstrong women 140
What duty they do owe their lords and husbands.

Widow

Come, come, you're mocking. We will have no telling.

Petruchio

Come on, I say, and first begin with her.

Widow

She shall not.

Petruchio

I say she shall.—And first begin with her. 145

Katherina

Fie, fie! Unknit that threat'ning unkind brow [2]
And dart not scornful glances from those eyes
To wound thy lord, thy king, thy governor.
stains/fields It blots° thy beauty as frosts do bite the meads,°
Confounds thy fame [3] as whirlwinds shake fair buds, 150
appropriate And in no sense is meet° or amiable.

1   *none so dry or thirsty*

     **I.e., there is no one so parched or
     thirsty who**

2   *foul contending*

     Vile combative

angry	A woman moved° is like a fountain troubled,
ugly/foul	Muddy, ill-seeming,° thick,° bereft of beauty,
	And, while it is so, none so dry or thirsty[1]
	Will deign to sip or touch one drop of it. 155
	Thy husband is thy lord, thy life, thy keeper,
	Thy head, thy sovereign, one that cares for thee,
	And, for thy maintenance, commits his body
	To painful labor both by sea and land,
be awake through	To watch° the night in storms, the day in cold, 160
	Whilst thou liest warm at home, secure and safe,
payment	And craves no other tribute° at thy hands
	But love, fair looks, and true obedience—
	Too little payment for so great a debt.
	Such duty as the subject owes the prince, 165
	Even such a woman oweth to her husband.
willful/obstinate	And when she is froward,° peevish,° sullen, sour,
	And not obedient to his honest will,
	What is she but a foul contending[2] rebel
sinful	And graceless° traitor to her loving lord? 170
foolish	I am ashamed that women are so simple°
	To offer war where they should kneel for peace,
influence	Or seek for rule, supremacy, and sway°
	When they are bound to serve, love, and obey.
	Why are our bodies soft and weak and smooth, 175
Unfit	Unapt° to toil and trouble in the world,
temperaments	But that our soft conditions° and our hearts
	Should well agree with our external parts?
feeble	Come, come, you froward and unable° worms!
proud	My mind hath been as big° as one of yours, 180
perhaps	My heart as great, my reason haply° more,
exchange	To bandy° word for word and frown for frown.
	But now I see our lances are but straws,
i.e., weak as straws	Our strength as weak,° our weakness past compare,

1   *vail your stomachs*

Surrender your pride

2   *In token*

As a sign

3   *do him ease*

Give him pleasure

4   *go thy ways*

I.e., well done

5   *shalt ha 't*

Will have it (the prize)

6   *good hearing*

A fine thing to hear

7   *the white*

**I.e., the bull's-eye, punning on
Bianca's name ("white," in Italian)**

8   *being a winner*

While I am ahead

_In_　　That° seeming to be most which we indeed least are. 185

use　　Then vail your stomachs,[1] for it is no boot,°

　　　　And place your hands below your husband's foot,

　　　　In token[2] of which duty, if he please,

　　　　My hand is ready. May it do him ease.[3]

Petruchio

Why, there's a wench! Come on and kiss me, Kate. 190

Lucentio

Well, go thy ways,[4] old lad, for thou shalt ha 't.[5]

Vincentio

obedient　　'Tis a good hearing[6] when children are toward.°

Lucentio

willful　　But a harsh hearing when women are froward.°

Petruchio

Come, Kate, we'll to bed.

　　　　[_to_ **Lucentio** _and_ **Hortensio**] We three are married, but

i.e., out of luck　　you two are sped.° 195

　　　　'Twas I won the wager, though you hit the white,[7]

　　　　And, being a winner,[8] God give you good night!

　　　　　　　　　　　　　　Petruchio [_and_ **Katherina**] _exit._

Hortensio

quarrelsome　　Now, go thy ways; thou hast tamed a curst° shrew.

Lucentio

'Tis a wonder, by your leave, she will be tamed so.

　　　　　　　　　　　　　　　　　　[_They exit._]

1   *I think he's starved by this*

       **I would think he had died by this
       time.**

2   *murrain*

       **Literally, a contagious and deadly
       disease of sheep or cattle, like
       anthrax; here, a metaphor for a
       terrible headache (from too much
       drink)**

Appendix:
The Taming of A Shrew

In the 1594 The Taming of A Shrew, *after the "taming" plot is concluded and the characters have left the stage, the following appears:*

> Then enter two bearing of **Sly** in his own apparel again, and leaves him where they found him, and then goes out.
> Then enter the **Tapster**.

Tapster
Now that the darksome night is overpast,
And dawning day appears in crystal sky,
Now must I haste abroad. But soft, who's this?
What, Sly? O wondrous, hath he lain here all night?
I'll wake him; I think he's starved by this [1]   5
But that his belly was so stuffed with ale.
What now, Sly, awake for shame!

Sly
give us Sim, gi's° some more wine. What's all the players
gone? Am not I a lord?

Tapster
A lord with a murrain.[2] Come, art thou drunken still?   10

Sly
Who's this? Tapster? O Lord, sirrah, I have had the
most remarkable bravest° dream tonight that ever thou heardest in all
thy life.

Tapster
Ay, marry, but you had best get you home, for your
beat wife will course° you for dreaming here tonight.   15

Sly
Will she? I know now how to tame a shrew:

1 *An if*

   If

2 Exeunt omnes.

   They all exit (Latin)

I dreamt upon it all this night till now,
And thou hast waked me out of the best dream
That ever I had in my life. I'll to my
Wife presently° and tame her too
An if¹ she'll anger me.

right now

20

Tapster

Nay tarry, Sly, for I'll go home with thee,
And hear the rest that thou hast dreamt tonight.

*Exeunt omnes.*²

Longer Notes

PAGE 45

Induction, 1.1.0   *Induction*
Shakespeare conceived these
introductory scenes about
Christopher Sly and the trick
played to convince him that he
is a great lord with an apt comic
touch that is almost always
succesful on stage, but in the
First Folio text Sly disappears
from the play after Act One,
scene one. Considering Shakespeare's usual care in resolving
all the plots of his plays (as, for
example, in the return of the
fairies at the end of *A Midsummer
Night's Dream*), some scholars
speculate that the text we have
is corrupt.

     Beginning with Alexan-
der Pope in 1723, editors have
often added to Shakespeare's
play *The Taming of the Shrew*
scenes taken from another,
anonymous comedy printed
in 1594 called *The Taming of a
Shrew*—a practice sometimes
adopted in the theater as
well. Because of its similarity
to Shakespeare's play in plot
and structure, scholars have
debated whether Shakespeare
had any hand in the writing of *A
Shrew* (see Editing *The Taming of
the Shrew*, p. 299). Whatever the
truth, the presence of Christopher Sly onstage, commenting
on the action throughout *The
Taming of a Shrew*, makes for a
more satisfactory development
and resolution of this plot than
that found in Shakespeare's
play. But when Sly awakens
from his supposed dream at the

end of *A Shrew* to announce that
he has learned "how to tame
a shrew" (see Appendix, page
289), his words would tend to
reduce the thematic richness
of Shakespeare's play to something of a how-to manual on
wife taming.

PAGE 69

1.1.0   **Tranio**

Tranio is a stock comic character,
the witty servant or slave of
the Italian dramatic tradition.
Typically cleverer than his master,
this character orchestrates the
intrigues that allow his master
to win the love of the heroine.
Shakespeare's portrayal of
Tranio, however, seems to reflect
tensions in the early modern
English system of service. An
apparently genuine affection
between Lucentio and Tranio
makes their relationship seem
more like friendship than a
function of the bonds of obligation and economic dependence
on which service relations
normally depended. Although
this idealization may have suited
English sensibilities by making

service seem to be a mutually
beneficial relation, Tranio's
cleverness in impersonating
Lucentio creates a comic echo of
the threat to orderly patriarchal
hierarchy posed by Katherina.
Late in the play, impersonating
Lucentio, Tranio orders that
Vincentio be sent off to prison.
One might compare him to the
more literal-minded Grumio to
understand better the potential
threats to the social system
Tranio poses.

PAGE 125

2.1.120   *What dowry shall I have
with her to wife*

Marriage was primarily an
economic and/or dynastic
arrangement in early modern
England. This does not mean
that love was irrelevant, but it
would not have been the only
motivation for this important
social institution. It was
assumed that love would follow
a marriage carried out with
proper consideration for all
involved. Petruchio here wants
to know what Katherina's family
will offer, but follows by

indicating what he will provide for her.

Under the system of primogeniture, the bulk of a man's inheritance would pass to his firstborn son and not his daughters, so the marriage contract was often a way of fathers providing for the welfare of beloved daughters. Although Baptista does not have any sons to inherit from him, and we might presume his estate will pass to one or both of his daughters, still the talk of dowry, widowhood, and contract that informs this dialogue would not have been unusual. In families that could afford it, some type of cash settlement or economic promise would have accompanied a woman into marriage. In the event of her husband's death, a widow would be entitled to a certain portion of her husband's estate, her dower—a legal provision meant to prevent her from falling into indigence or having to depend on her children and relatives for support. All this would be specified by legal contract between the wife's family and the family of the husband (or the husband himself). In this particular case, Petruchio's offer of *all* his lands and leases, should he die before Katherina, seems remarkably generous, a dower to which he was not obligated either by law or custom.

What is unusual—and, certainly for a modern audience, disturbing—in this exchange between Baptista and Petruchio is that neither seems to pay more than lip service to Katherina's wishes. If marriage in the period was a system of economic and social alliances, negotiations for it were nevertheless expected to take into consideration the feelings of all parties, and Katherina is not consulted here or anywhere else.

PAGE 131

2.1.185   *for you are called plain Kate*

The initial interview between Katherina and Petruchio is framed by two speeches in which he gives Katherina a new name and, ostensibly, a new role to play. Instead of Katherina she becomes Kate, and he makes a significant pun on *cates*, meaning small cakes or sweets. She is something fine and dainty, but also something to be displayed or consumed, presumably for Petruchio's pleasure. At the end of this interview Petruchio promises to "tame" Katherina and turn her "from a wild Kate"—with a pun on *wildcat*—into a "Kate / Conformable as other household Kates" (2.1.269–271). She may be fine and dainty, but he suggests that she belongs primarily inside the household. His words promise an extraordinary constriction of her freedom, removing her from the public sphere ("the prettiest Kate in Christendom") to the domestic one ("as other household Kates").

In traditional cottage industries of early modern England, women took public roles as retailers of goods produced in the household, goods that were sold from the house. Ironically, however, with the growth of commerce in late 16th- and early 17th-century England, business took place increasingly outside the household and became almost completely associated with men. Women were more and more consigned to duties within a home conceived of as private, domestic space. Something of this transformation is reflected in *The Taming of the Shrew*. Men such as Baptista and Vincentio clearly conduct public business, whereas Bianca and Katherina are expected to stay at home, where they are schooled in poetry, the arts, and, presumably, feminine modesty. Kate's identification as a shrew has something to do with her insistence on maintaining a public persona. (See Korda in For Further Reading.)

PAGE 165

3.2.41   *Why, Petruchio is coming*
What follows is one of the most difficult passages in the play. The description seems to provide a key to Petruchio's taming methods. Petruchio arrives at his wedding fantastically dressed and riding an old,

diseased horse, which Biondello
describes in grotesque detail.
The elaborate description seems
consistent with a pattern of
images throughout the play,
but it cannot be interpreted in
relation to this pattern in any
obvious way. Perhaps Petruchio rides an old, lame horse
to symbolize his mastery of
Katherina, the "hilding" (see
note at 2.1.26) that must be put
into proper service. Or perhaps
Petruchio parodies a *charivari*,
or skimmington ride, a highly
theatrical ritual of rural England,
as a reminder to Katherina and all
concerned of what may happen
to him if he fails to control his
wife. In the skimmington, a
neighbor might dress as the
offending husband and ride
backward through town on a
horse, symbolizing the inver-
sion of order in the household.
In a general way, Biondello's
fantastic description seems to
allude to the monstrous parody
of marriage that Katherina and
Petruchio's match will become
if one or indeed both of them do
not change.

THE
Taming of the Shrew.

Actus primus. Scœna Prima.

Enter Begger and Hostes, Christophero Sly.

Begger.

Le pheeze you infaith.

Host. A paire of stockes you rogue.

Beg. Y'are a baggage, the *Slies* are no
Rogues, Looke in the Chronicles, we came
in with *Richard Conqueror*: therefore *Paucas pallabris*, let the world slide: Sessa.

Host. You will not pay for the glasses you haue burst?

Beg. No, not a deniere: go by S. *Ieronimie*, goe to thy
cold bed, and warme thee.

Host. I know my remedie, I must go fetch the Headborough.

Beg. Third, or fourth, or fift Borough, Ile answere
him by Law, Ile not budge an inch boy: Let him come,
and kindly. *Falles asleepe.*

Winde hornes. Enter a Lord from hunting, with his traine.

Lo. Huntsman I charge thee, tender wel my hounds,
Brach *Meriman*, the poore Curre is imbost,
And couple *Clowder* with the deepe-mouth'd brach,
Saw'st thou not boy how *Siluer* made it good
At the hedge corner, in the couldest fault,
I would not loose the dogge for twentie pound.

Huntf. Why *Belman* is as good as he my Lord,
He cried vpon it at the meerest losse,
And twice to day pick'd out the dullest sent,
Trust me, I take him for the better dogge.

Lord. Thou art a Foole, if *Eccho* were as fleete,
I would esteeme him worth a dozen such:
But sup them well, and looke vnto them all,
To morrow I intend to hunt againe.

Huntf. I will my Lord.

Lord. What's heere? One dead, or drunke? See doth
he breath?

2. Hun. He breath's my Lord. Were he not warm'd
with Ale, this were a bed but cold to sleep so soundly.

Lord. Oh monstrous beast, how like a swine he lyes,
Grim death, how foule and loathsome is thine image:
Sirs, I will practise on this drunken man.
What thinke you, if he were conuey'd to bed,
Wrap'd in sweet cloathes: Rings put vpon his fingers:
A most delicious banquet by his bed,
And braue attendants neere him when he wakes,
Would not the begger then forget himselfe?

1. Hun. Beleeue me Lord, I thinke he cannot choose.

2. H. It would seem strange vnto him when he wak'd

Lord. Euen as a flatt'ring dreame, or worthlesse fancie.

Then take him vp, and manage well the iest:
Carrie him gently to my fairest Chamber,
And hang it round with all my vvanton pictures:
Balme his foule head in warme distilled waters,
And burne sweet Wood to make the Lodging sweete:
Procure me Musicke readie when he vvakes,
To make a dulcet and a heauenly sound:
And if he chance to speake, be readie straight
(And with a lowe submissiue reuerence)
Say, what is it your Honor vvil command:
Let one attend him vvith a siluer Bason
Full of Rose-water, and bestrew'd with Flowers,
Another beare the Ewer: the third a Diaper,
And say wilt please your Lordship coole your hands,
Some one be readie with a costly suite,
And aske him what apparrel he will weare:
Another tell him of his Hounds and Horse,
And that his Ladie mournes at his disease,
Perswade him that he hath bin Lunaticke,
And when he sayes he is, say that he dreames,
For he is nothing but a mightie Lord:
This do, and do it kindly, gentle sirs,
It wil be pastime passing excellent,
If it be husbanded with modestie.

1. Hunts. My Lord I warrant you we wil play our part
As he shall thinke by our true diligence
He is no lesse then what we say he is.

Lord. Take him vp gently, and to bed with him,
And each one to his office when he wakes. *Sound trumpets.*

Sirrah, go see what Trumpet 'tis that sounds,
Belike some Noble Gentleman that meanes
(Trauelling some iourney) to repose him heere.

Enter Seruingman.

How now? who is it?

Ser. An't please your Honor, Players
That offer seruice to your Lordship.

Enter Players.

Lord. Bid them come neere:
Now fellowes, you are welcome.

Players. We thanke your Honor.

Lord. Do you intend to stay with me to night?

2. Player. So please your Lordshippe to accept our
dutie.

Lord. With all my heart. This fellow I remember,
Since once he plaide a Farmers eldest sonne,
'Twas where you woo'd the Gentlewoman so well:
I haue forgot your name: but sure that part

W 25

Editing *The Taming of the Shrew*
by David Scott Kastan

The earliest text of *The Taming of the Shrew* is that which was published in the Folio of 1623, though the play is actually one of Shakespeare's earliest comedies, probably written sometime around 1592. In the Folio, it is printed as the eleventh play in the section of Comedies, appearing between *As You Like It* and *All's Well That Ends Well*. The text seems to have been printed from a manuscript, possibly authorial, but one that seems to have been somewhat carelessly prepared (on the evidence of the seeming omission of a number of small words and some confusions in the speech prefixes, though these could be errors introduced in the printing house).

Complicating our understanding of the text of the play is the existence of a quarto playbook published anonymously in 1594, *The Taming of A Shrew*. *A Shrew* has all the plot elements of Shakespeare's play (though it completes the play's frame, with Sly reappearing at the end; see Appendix, page 289). It sets the main action in Greece rather than Italy and therefore uses different names. It is shorter than Shakespeare's play, and, while *A Shrew* borrows lines from other Elizabethan plays, it shares very few complete lines with *The Shrew*. Initially scholars assumed the cruder *A Shrew* was simply the source for Shakespeare's play; then it become fashionable to argue that *A Shrew* was a so-called "bad" quarto, a version compiled perhaps by actors inaccurately recalling Shakespeare's play; now many scholars believe that both the anonymous *A Shrew* and Shakespeare's play as it is printed in the Folio derive from a version by Shakespeare now lost: *A Shrew* representing some kind of derivative of Shakespeare's play, and the Folio *The Taming of The Shrew* a revision of Shakespeare's earlier version (though perhaps one still incomplete on the evidence of some loose ends that normally pass unnoticed on the stage).

In general, the editorial work of this present edition is conservative, preserving and clarifying the text that appears in the Folio, emending only when it is manifestly in error (and recording these changes in the Textual Notes). The occasional lines in Latin or Italian are here corrected, as it seems implausible that the errors are intended since they would be almost impossible to recognize on stage. All other changes to the Folio text are in accord with modern practices of editing Shakespeare: normalizing spelling, capitalization, and punctuation, removing superfluous italics, regularizing the names of characters, and rationalizing entrances and exits. Editorial stage directions are kept to a minimum and added always in brackets.

A comparison of the edited text of the Induction, scene 1, lines 1–83 with the facsimile page of the Folio (on p. 298) reveals many of the issues in this process of editing. The speech prefixes are expanded for clarity, so that *Host.* becomes **Hostess** and *Lo.* becomes **Lord**. The Folio's speech prefix *Beg.* is not expanded to **Beggar** but consistently given as **Sly**, on the principle of identifying characters by name if it is clearly given, as in the Induction, scene 2, lines 5 and 17–18.

The kind of substantive change that is made to the Folio can be seen in line 9, where the Folio text reads "I must go fetch the thirdborough." The Folio has in place of the unfamiliar final word, "Headborough." The words were synonyms, each meaning "constable," but that Shakespeare intended "thirdborough," an emendation first proposed in the early eighteenth century, is made clear by the line that follows: "Third, or fourth, or fifthborough, I'll answer him by law," which makes sense only if the Folio's reading is corrected.

Normally, however, changes to the Folio text are matters only of modernization. Spelling throughout is regularized to reflect modern spelling practices. As spelling in Shakespeare's time had not yet been standardized, words were spelled in various ways that indicated their proximate pronunciation, and compositors, in any case, were under no obligation to follow the spelling of their copy. Little, then, is to be gained in an edition such as this by following the spelling of the original printed text. Therefore "paire" unproblematically becomes "pair" in 1.1.2; "goe" becomes "go" in line 7 (though, as a sign of how inconsistent early modern spelling was, note that "go" earlier in the line is spelled as it would be today); and "wel" becomes "well" in line 12. As these indicate, old spellings are consistently modernized, but old *forms* of words (e.g., "thee" in line 12; "Saw'st" in line 15) are retained. The capitalized first letters of many nouns in the Folio (e.g., "Chronicles" in line 4) are reduced to lower case, except where modern punctuation would demand them. The superfluous italics of proper names (e.g., "*Clowder*" and "*Siluer*" in lines 14 and 15) are all removed. Punctuation, too, is adjusted to reflect modern practice (which is designed to clarify the logical relations between grammatical units, unlike seventeenth-century punctuation, which was dominated by rhythmical concerns), since the punctuation is no more likely than the spelling or capitalization to be Shakespeare's own. Thus, in the Folio the Lord's plan for the drunken Sly reads:

> What thinke you, if he were conuey'd to bed,
> Wrap'd in sweet cloathes: Ringes put vpon his fingers :
> A most delicious banquet by his bed,
> And brave attendants neere him when he wakes,
> Would not the begger then forget himselfe?

Modernized this reads:

> What think you? If he were conveyed to bed,
> Wrapped in sweet clothes, rings put upon his fingers,
> A most delicious banquet by his bed,
> And brave attendants near him when he wakes,
> Would not the beggar then forget himself?
>
> (Induction, scene 1, 33–37)

No doubt there is some loss in this modernization. Clarity and consistency are gained at the expense of some loss of expressive detail, but normalizing spelling, capitalization, and punctuation allows the text to be read with far greater ease than the original, and essentially as it was intended to be understood. Seventeenth-century readers would have been unsurprised to find "u" for "v" in "conuey'd (conveyed) in line 33 or "v"" for "u" in "vpon"" in line 34, nor would they have been confused by the spellings "neere" or "begger." The intrusive "e"s in words like "himselfe" (line 37) or "Ringes" (line 34) would not have seemed odd, nor would the "literary" capitalization of the noun. The colons in line 34 mark a somewhat heavier pause than the commas that follow but don't define a different grammatical relation as they would in modern usage. Modernizing in all these cases clarifies rather than alters Shakespeare's intentions. If in modernization we do lose the historical feel of the text Shakespeare's contemporaries read, it is important to note that Shakespeare's contemporaries would not have thought the Folio in any sense archaic or quaint, as these details inevitably make it for a reader today. The text would have seemed to them as modern as this one does to us. Indeed, many of the Folio's typographical peculiarities are the result of its effort to make the printed page look up-to-date for potential buyers.

Modern readers, however, cannot help but be distracted by the different conventions they encounter on the Folio page. While it is indeed of interest to see how orthography and typography have changed over time, these changes are not primary concerns for most readers of this edition. What little, then, is lost in a careful modernization of the text is more than made up for by the removal of the artificial obstacle of unfamiliar spelling forms and punctuation habits, which neither Shakespeare nor his publishers could have intended as interpretive difficulties for his readers.

Textual Notes

The list below records all substantive departures in this edition from the Folio text of 1623. It does not record modernizations of spelling, corrections of obvious typographical errors, adjustments of lineation, rationalizations of speech prefixes (SP), minor repositioning or rewording of stage directions (SD), or the correction of the few Latin and Italian phrases spoken by characters. The adopted reading in this edition is given first in boldface and followed by the original, rejected reading of the Folio, or noted as being absent from the Folio text. Editorial stage directions are not collated but are enclosed within brackets in the text. Latin stage directions are translated (e.g., *They all exit* for *Exeunt omnes*), as are the Latin act and scene designations of the Folio (e.g., Act 1, scene 1 for *Actus primus, scena prima*) and are supplied where they are missing or misplaced.

Ind. 1.0SD Enter Sly and the Hostess. Enter Begger and Hostes, Christophero Sly; **Ind. 1.1SP Sly** Beg. [and throughout Induction]; **Ind. 1.9 thirdborough** Headborough; **Ind. 1.13 Breathe** Brach; **Ind. 1.79SP A Player** 2. Player; **Ind. 1. 85SP A Player** Sincklo; **Ind. 2. 18 Sly's** Sies; **Ind. 2.22 fourteen pence** xiiii d.; **Ind. 2.98 lose** loose; **Ind. 2.99SP Page** Lady [and throughout Induction].

1.1.3 for fore; **1.1.24 satiety** sacietie; **1.1.46SD suitor** sister; **1.1.106 There! Love** Their Love; **1.1.204 colored** Conlord; **1.1.235 would** could;

1.1.240 **your** you; 1.1.244SD **speak** speakes; 1.2.18 **masters** mistris; 1.2.31 **pip** peepe; 1.2.49 **grows. But** growes but; 1.2.70 **she as** she is as; 1.2.117 **me and other** me. Other; 1.2.168 **me** one; 1.2.186 **Antonio's** Butonios; 1.2.262 **feat** seeke

2.1.8 **thee** [not in F]; 2.1.75–76 **wooing. Neighbor** wooing neighbors; 2.1.79 **you** [not in F]; 2.1.186 **bonny** bony; 2.1.198 **joint** ioyn'd; 2.1.241 **askance** a sconce

3.1.45–48 [assigned to Lucentio in F]; 3.1.49SP **Bianca** [not in F]; 3.1.50SP **Lucentio** Bian.; 3.1.52SP **Bianca** Hort.; 3.1.72 **A re** Are; 3.1.73 **B mi** Beeme; 3.1.74 **C fa ut** C favt; 3.1.76 **E la** Ela; 3.1.79 **change** charge; 3.1.79 **odd** old; 3.1.80SP **Messenger** Nicke; 3.2.16 **Make feasts, invite friends** Make friends, invite; 3.2.29 **thy** [not in F]; 3.2.30 **old** [not in F]; 3.2.33 **hear** heard; 3.2.52 **swayed** Waid; 3.2.124 **to** [not in F]; 3.2.195SP **Gremio** Gra

4.1.23SP **Curtis** Gru.; 4.1.41 **their white** the white; 4.1.102SP **Grumio** Gre.; 4.1.133 **off** of; 4.1.182 **ate** eate; 4.2.4SP **Hortensio** Luc.; 4.2.6SP **and 8SP Lucentio** Hor.; 4.2.13 **none** me; 4.2.31 **her** them; 4.2.72 **Take in . . . alone** Take me . . . alone [assigned to Par. in F]; 4.2.72SD **Merchant** Pedant [and throughout]; 4.3.48 **to** too; 4.3.63SP **Haberdasher** Fel.; 4.3.81 **a** [not in F]; 4.3.88 **a** [not in F]; 4.4.0SD **booted and bareheaded** [after line 18 in F]; 4.4.1 **Sir** Sirs; 4.4.5 **Where . . . Pegasus** [assigned to Tranio in F]; 4.4.77 **he's** has; 4.4.88 **except** expect; 4.5.19 **is** in; 4.5.39 **Whither** Whether; 4.5.39 **where** whether; 4.5.80 **be** [not in F]

5.1.5 **master's** mistris; 5.1.24 **to** from; 5.1.44 **master's** Mistris; 5.2.2 **done** come; 5.2.38 **thee** the; 5.2.46 **bitter** better; 5.2.66 **for** sir; 5.2.138 **one** fiue

The Taming of the Shrew on the Early Stage
by Nicholas F. Radel

f *The Taming of the Shrew* seems troubling to the modern reader because its story of wife-taming is offensive, onstage it is a fast-paced comedy that brilliantly exploits the theatrical conventions of the Elizabethan playhouse—not the famous Globe Theatre, which Shakespeare's company built in 1599, but probably its predecessor, called simply the Theatre. Like the Globe, the Theatre was a polygonal building open to the sky, and its name too alluded to the world itself, in this case the earthly stage on which people play their parts. Three galleries lined the inside wall of the building, where the better sort of people sat. In the center was the yard where, for a penny (a not inconsiderable sum), London's apprentices and maids, soldiers and prostitutes stood to watch the battle between Petruchio and Kate unfold. Just as Shakespeare's comedy depicted lords and beggars, men and women, masters and servants, the Theatre accommodated a huge cross section of Shakespeare's London. And because its immense stage (approximately forty feet wide by twenty-seven feet deep) was bare and devoid of scenery, this audience could be transported effortlessly from the English country pub, where the drunken Sly falls into a stupor, to Padua, center of learning in Italy.

At the rear of the stage the front wall of the tiring-house (the main storage area and dressing rooms) created a sounding board

Fig 1. In the large London playhouses, the balcony above the stage could be used for staging, seating, or to house musicians.

Fig 2. English Renaissance drama made minimal use of sets or backdrops. In the absence of a set, the stage pillars could be incorporated into the action, standing in for trees and other architectural elements.

Fig 3. The discovery space, located in the middle of the backstage wall, could be used as a third entrance as well as a location for scenes requiring special staging, such as in a tomb or bedchamber.

Fig 4. A trapdoor led to the area below the stage, known as "Hell" (as contrasted with the painted ceiling, known as "Heaven" or the "heavens"). Ghosts or other supernatural figures could descend through the trap, and it could also serve as a grave.

that could be painted or covered with a decorative curtain called an arras. The tiring-house wall combined simplicity with versatility, for it included several doors—two on the sides for entrances and exits—and perhaps a "discovery space" or (as some scholars believe) another door in the middle that opened to reveal surprising scenes that would then move forward onto the stage proper. In *The Shrew*, any of these doors could have played a part in the action. "Knock me here," Petruchio tells Grumio, and the presence of a large door on stage gives the lie to the servant's amusing failure to grasp his master's meaning. The tiring house doors may have opened suddenly to reveal a pathetic "Litio," carrying—or wearing around his neck—the lute that Katherina has broken on his head. Or they might stand resolutely closed to Vincentio when he tries to gain entrance to his son's house.

Just above the doors, the second level of the seating gallery extended behind the stage, and audience members might sit here, creating a performance in the round. But this space, or some temporary platform adjacent to it, could also be used for staging scenes. It is probably from here that the hungover Sly watches Petruchio tame Kate, and where he falls asleep. Shakespeare's audience would always be looking across the stage to some other part of the audience, for the auditorium was open to the sky and performances took place in the afternoon. When we say, then, that the Induction reminds the audience that it is watching a play, the point is literal—for spectators watch Sly over the heads of the other actors on stage, and he is watching the same play about Katherina and Petruchio that they are. This was one way Shakespeare blurred the line between the world of the play and the real world, leading the audience to wonder whether the story of Katherina's taming is little more than fantasy.

Shakespeare's actors would have worn ornate, colorful costumes that emblematically represented their character or status. These costumes would most likely have been fashionable clothes of the time period, whether Elizabethan or Italian (as Italian clothes were very fashionable in Shakespeare's England). But they would not have been exclusively or specifically Italian. That is, they would not have contributed to a realistic signification of place. Lucentio would have been dressed fashionably as a wealthy merchant's son and Tranio in the plainer clothes of a servant. When they exchange clothes, Tranio would not only seem to be his own master but engaging (as Vincentio fears) in a criminal trespass by impersonating his betters.

As there was also no scenery, Shakespeare established time and place through words. When Lucentio first enters, he immediately comments on "the great desire" he has "[t]o see fair Padua" (1.1.1–2). And, later, when Grumio returns to Petruchio's country house after the long journey from his master's wedding, the season itself changes to reflect his mood: "my very lips might freeze to my teeth," he says, "ere I should come by a fire to thaw me" (4.1.5–8). Shakespeare creates setting in the mind of the spectator, which allows the action to move with great fluidity from one place to another. In *The Taming of the Shrew* Shakespeare uses this fluidity specifically to help underline the farce.

For example, late in Act Four, in one scene Tranio introduces the Merchant disguised as Vincentio to Baptista in Padua, and, in another scene, Petruchio and Katherina begin their journey to her father's house. The scenes reflect each other thematically: the young men are busy fooling Baptista, convincing him one man is another, just at the moment when Petruchio insists that Kate call the sun the moon—a sun that, weather permitting, the audience would see shining just above their heads. The rapid shift from scene to scene throughout this act would create an impression that the world of the play was quickly becoming disordered. Then, into this mix, Shakespeare introduces the real Vincentio, on his way to Padua, but not before he is greeted as a young, budding maiden by Kate and Petruchio. The more quickly these absurd juxtapositions occur, the more they create the hilarious impression of an impending explosion.

For all its fast-paced intrigues, quarrels, beatings, and journeys, *The Taming of the Shrew*, like all of Shakespeare's plays, is as much about words as action. One did not go to see a play in Shakespeare's time so much as one went to hear it, much as today we go to hear an opera. Like the tenor who sings a role, an actor on Shakespeare's stage "personated," or impersonated someone, and his primary tool was language. Notwithstanding the immense pleasure of the spoken word written by as gifted a poet as Shakespeare, the general effect would have been to emphasize the actors' playing their roles. More significant, it may have suggested that in life one had to find the proper role to play as each occasion demanded.

In Act Four, scene five, when Katherina, following Petruchio's lead, addresses Vincentio as a "[Y]oung budding virgin, fair and fresh and sweet," the wily Petruchio suddenly shifts purpose: "Why, how now, Kate! I hope thou art not mad" (38, 43). It is a moment of truth in which Katherina might throw up her arms in desperation, but instead she focuses all her intelligence and wit into a new role: "Pardon, old father, my mistaking eyes / That have been so bedazzled with the sun" (46–47). Not mad, she says, but blinded by the light, which has so recently changed from moon to sun. She brilliantly fashions herself anew within the drama her husband is writing extempore before her eyes. At this moment, Katherina and Petruchio do not, as the cliché goes, "speak the same language." They speak language the same way. An Elizabethan audience would perhaps have been aware of and pleased by those variations in rhetoric and meaning that helped establish the "personation" that was taking place before them.

Which brings us to that most alien and difficult convention of Shakespeare's stage: the boy actor. All parts on Shakespeare's stage would have been played by males, with female roles going to younger men who had not yet acquired beards or who were especially adept at playing women. There is no reason to imagine that young men could not convincingly impersonate women. When Lucentio falls head over heels in love at first sight, the audience would have taken at face value the ability of the actor playing Bianca to look attractive in a woman's dress and makeup and to express himself convincingly. Nevertheless, as he does with other stage conventions, Shakespeare could play with this one to create particular meanings. In the Induction, for example, the Page Barthol'mew dresses as a woman and pretends to be Sly's wife. The illusion is so convincing that Sly invites "her" to bed with him. Barthol'mew excuses "herself" because in this case we know that "she" is really a he, and the intimation of sexual activity between the two men becomes a kind of joke at Sly's expense.

But this example might lead us to look closer at Kate. In her case, Shakespeare does not explicitly call attention to the actor beneath the costume, but Katherina as written is clearly a figure of gender transgression. In her outrageous words, bold public behavior, and physical violence, she usurps qualities usually reserved for men. In comparison to the modest and reticent Bianca, Kate seems as rough and tumble as Petruchio, and it is entirely possible that the actor playing her may have communicated through his own male body something of the verbal and physical freedoms typically accorded men. What happens to her by the end of the play, however, is significant: she still speaks fluently and articulately, but now she speaks to women and defers to men. And she is rewarded with something Shakespeare would not allow Barthol'mew earlier: a kiss. We might imagine that the boy actor now communicates something very different by downplaying his own male body to reveal Katherina as a woman, which is, the final line says, a real "wonder."

Significant Performances
by Nicholas F. Radel

1590s   We assume that Shakespeare's version of *The Taming of the Shrew* was performed in London shortly after it was written, probably sometime in the early 1590s. Nevertheless, the diary of theatrical manager Philip Henslowe provides the first recorded performance of what may have been Shakespeare's play on tour at Newington Butts: June 13, 1594.

1611–1633   John Fletcher wrote *The Woman's Prize; or the Tamer Tamed*, a sequel to Shakespeare's play in 1611, so we can speculate that *The Taming of the Shrew* was popular throughout Shakespeare's lifetime. According to the title page of the 1631 Quarto edition of *The Shrew*, the play was acted by the King's Men at both the Globe and the Blackfriar's theatres, which the King's Men began using regularly in 1610.

1633   On November 26, 1633, the King's Men performed the play at court before King Charles I and Queen Henrietta Maria. Two days later, they performed *The Woman's Prize*. According to the Master of the Revels, Sir Henry Herbert, Shakespeare's play was "liked," but Fletcher's "very well liked."

1663–1664   The Master of the Revels records a performance by Thomas Killigrew's company, the King's Company, of a "Revived Play Taminge the Shrew." If the reference is to Shakespeare's play, it is the last recorded performance of the play as Shakespeare wrote it until 1844.

1667–1756   The diarist Samuel Pepys attended a performance of *The Taming of a Shrew* on April 9, and again on November 1, 1667. Although he thought it "but mean," the play that he saw was John Lacy's *Sauny the Scot: or, The Taming of the Shrew,* a prose adaptation of Shakespeare's play written in 1667 and first published in 1698. *Sauny* follows the outline of Shakespeare's taming plot, but the play's shrew, Margaret, doesn't capitulate easily. As late as Act Five she threatens Petruchio: "I will learn to rail at thee in all languages; thunder shall be soft music to my tongue." And he, in response, devises sensational new trials: he threatens to have one of her teeth pulled and to have her buried alive. *Sauny the Scott* was frequently revived, appearing last on the London stage in 1736. (See Inspired by *The Taming of the Shrew*.)

1754–1897   In 1754, the great actor and theatrical manager David Garrick adapted Shakespeare's play into *Catharine and Petruchio,* published in 1756. Designed as an afterpiece to a more substantial entertainment, *Catharine and Petruchio* is only three acts long. Without the balance provided by the more subtle comedy of Shakespeare's subplots (which Garrick omitted), the story of *Catharine and Petruchio* seems little more than farce. Nevertheless, produced in the age of sensibility, Garrick wrings from it a good deal of sentiment: Garrick's Catharine is drawn to Petruchio from the first, and once she proves herself to be a dutiful wife, Petruchio vows that he shall "doff the [role of] lordly husband." *Catharine and Petruchio* was performed in England and America for well over 100 years by some of the finest actors of the time: Sarah Siddons and J. P. Kemble played the roles in 1788, and Charles Macready performed in the play as late as 1842. The promptbook for Kemble's performance records for the first time a bit of stage business that became traditional: Petruchio's brandishing a whip onstage. Still, during the late eighteenth century, actresses playing Catharine tended to represent her in a dignified manner befitting a woman of her position, while actors portrayed Petruchio as polite but able to assert control. Although *The Taming of the Shrew* (in this non-Shakespearean version) became one of the most popular of Shakespeare's plays during the period, George Bernard Shaw perhaps aptly labeled Garrick's play a "puerile and horribly caddish knockabout farce." (See Inspired by *The Taming of the Shrew*.)

1844   Encouraged by J.R. Planché, who supervised the production, Benjamin Webster, manager of the Haymarket Theatre, London, revived *The Taming of the Shrew* substantially as Shakespeare wrote it for the first time since the seventeenth century. In a revolutionary departure from usual nineteenth-century practice, Planché had the players perform for Sly on a bare platform set up for the occasion, using no additional scenery except screens and curtains. Planché's and Webster's innovations in staging anticipated some of the key strategies for staging Shakespeare's plays in the twentieth century.

1856   Samuel Phelps opened a more scenically elaborate production of Shakespeare's *The Taming of the Shrew* at the Sadler's Well's Theatre. A success with its audience, Phelps's production of Shakespeare's play still did little to convince critics used to Garrick's version that *The Taming of the Shrew* was stageworthy.

1887   In a lavish and extremely important revival, the American theater producer Augustin Daly staged Shakespeare's play in a historically realistic style. Typical of Daly's scenic excess, indoor scenes were furnished with thick rugs and elaborately carved gold furniture reminiscent of early modern Italy. Nevertheless, the performance of two great American actors made this production pivotal in the history of the play. Ada Rehan played Katherina as a powerful and dignified shrew in a deep red dress and with a fiery-colored wig, while John Drew created a gentlemanly Petruchio. Together, they convinced playgoers and critics alike that Shakespeare's play is a rich comedy of character and not the farce that Garrick's version makes it out to be. Subsequent to Daly's production, revivals of Garrick's play both in England and the United States were infrequent and increasingly disliked.

1893   Heavily influenced by the farcical tradition of Garrick, Frank Benson staged his first production at the Memorial Theatre in Stratford-upon-Avon. Benson's productions relied on acrobatic physicality, but despite their old-fashioned adherence to slapstick, their design tended to be minimal rather than the elaborate staging of Daly and others in the nineteenth century. Thus, like Webster and Planché, Benson antici-pated an important development in twentieth-century design.

1905   In an interpretive move that would have tremendous influence on later interpretations of the play, two American actors, E. H. Southern and Julia Marlowe, combined farce with the comedy of character seen in Daly's production. Despite making the sentimental suggestion that Katherina learns to control her husband in a socially appropriate way over the course of the play, the production neverthe-less allowed both characters to engage in a great deal of rambunctious horseplay.

1913   Reacting to the elaborate scenery of the nineteenth-century stage, Martin Harvey was the first director to mount a successful production influenced by William Poel's theories about Elizabethan staging. Although Harvey hung tapestries of different colors to indicate changes in location and dropped in furniture from the fly space to create indoor settings, he followed Poel in using a plat-form stage that jutted into the audience to achieve continuous action onstage that paused only once, at intermission. Harvey's was the first performance of the play to interpolate the additional Christopher Sly scenes from the 1594 Quarto edition of *The Taming of a Shrew*.

1928   A prime innovator in the development of modern dress productions of Shakespeare, Barry Jackson emphasized the anachronistic differences between the characters' modern dress and the Elizabethan ideas they articulated. Photographers recorded Kather-ina and Petruchio's wedding, and the newlyweds returned to Padua in a motorcar. Ironically, Katherina delivered her final speech of submission in a sports blazer and skirt, wearing the fashionably bobbed hair of the 1920s.

1929   The first feature-length talking film of a Shakespearean play starred America's sweetheart, Mary Pickford, and her swashbuckling husband, Douglas Fairbanks. Helping repopularize wildly farcical interpretations of the play in the United States, producer Sam Taylor replaced large portions of Shakespeare's text with outrageous inventions such as a trained dog that "speaks" to Petruchio and dwarves that tumble down steps. In the film's most famous moment, Pickford winks at the audience after Katherina's final speech.

1931   The Old Vic, under the direction of Harcourt Williams, staged the first significant production of *The Shrew* in the style of the Italian commedia dell'arte. Wearing the brightly colored Italian costumes and masks of this tradition, the actors were distanced from the audience, making the conflict between Katherina and Petruchio seem more like spirited horseplay than troubling abuse.

1939   Russian émigré director Theodore Komisarjevsky mounted *The Taming of the Shrew* at the Memorial Theatre in Stratford-upon-Avon. Believing that directors should interpret rather than merely stage plays, Komisarjevsky set *The Shrew* among a series of classical pillars and arches painted in pinks, blues, yellows, and greens that communicated indifference to the play's specific time period and location. Characters were costumed in a variety of styles from the Restoration to the contemporary.

1948   Based on *The Taming of the Shrew*, Cole Porter's *Kiss Me, Kate*, with a libretto by Sam and Bella Spewack, ran for over 1,000 performances at the New Century Theater in New York. The Spewacks's inventive book creates a play-within-a-play about Fred Graham and Lilli Vanessi, two actors formerly married and now working out their own taming plot as the stars of a new musical version of *The Taming of the Shrew*. Porter's brilliant music and lyrics make the show worth studying alongside Shakespeare. (See Inspired by *The Taming of the Shrew*.)

1960   In an age of absurdist experimentation and existential anxiety, set designer Alix Stone revealed multiple layers of reality in John Barton's production of the play for the Royal Shakespeare Company. Stone set the Induction in a rural inn with multiple windows. The stage then revolved to reveal the space outside the inn, where the players performed the story of Katherina and Petruchio. Stressing the thematic significance of the Induction to the taming plot, Barton helped make it an essential part of subsequent performances.

1966   Set against the visually stunning, carnivalesque world of sixteenth-century Italy, director Franco Zeffirelli's lush film adaptation for Columbia Pictures starred Elizabeth Taylor and Richard Burton in a rough-and-tumble romance in which the loutish Petruchio's bullying of Katherina gives way to genuine passion on both sides. Much as nineteenth-century theatrical productions sacrificed Shakespeare's text to the demands of their extravagant staging, Zeffirelli's film cuts the poetry to make room for his splendid visual effects.

1967   Building on Barton's insights, Trevor Nunn brilliantly emphasized the varying thematic layers that make up Shakespeare's multiple-plotted play in his production for the Royal Shakespeare Company. Katherina and Petruchio fell in love within the framework of their own farcical play; that play was watched by Sly, who was performing in a play orchestrated by the Lord; and he was part of a play called *The Taming of the Shrew* staged by the Royal Shakespeare Company. At the end of the production, Sly seemed to awake from a dream less alive than he was while engaged in the vivid performance he has just seen.

1975   A symptom of a growing lack of sympathy with Shakespeare's play (brought on, in part, by the radical political movements of the era), Charles Marowitz's performance piece *The Shrew* examined the sadomasochistic implications of marriage in Shakespeare's time and our own. Marowitz showed Petruchio forcefully sodomizing Katherina and then prompting her as she makes her final speech. (See Inspired by *The Taming of the Shrew*.)

1976   A television adaptation of the American Conservatory Theater's commedia dell'arte production of *The Shrew* followed the tradition begun by Harcourt Williams at the Old Vic. A good example of a new trend in contemporary production, the strapping, bare-chested Marc Singer provided a distinctly modern motivation for Katherina's interest in Petruchio.

1978   In a disturbing reflection of feminist discomfort with the play, Michael Bogdanov's modern dress production for the Royal Shakespeare Company emphasized the similarities between Shakespeare's treatment of women and modern ones. Starring Jonathan Pryce, Bogdanov's production began when a drunken audience member yelled at an usher, expressing his disapproval that a woman was telling him what to do. Raging onto the stage, he initiated a brawl that destroyed the traditional set to reveal an abstract, modern industrial scene. The audience member, it turned out, was Christopher Sly, who was escorted off stage only to return as Petruchio, who then savagely tamed Katherina. Katherina's masochistic submission in this production helped popularize the idea that *The Taming of the Shrew* is a problematic and unpleasant play.

1978   Almost as if in response to English productions emphasizing the play's misogyny, the American producer Joseph Papp staged *The Taming of the Shrew* in Central Park with Meryl Streep and Raul Julia. In what seems to have become a dominant strategy in American productions of the play, Streep and Julia emphasized the main characters' genuine love for and duty to one another. "This is not," Streep said in the *New York Times*, "a sadomasochist show."

1980   Jonathan Miller's television production for the BBC Shakespeare series utilized early modern Italian settings and costumes to emphasize the historical specificity of Shakespeare's play and its theme of female obedience to male authority. Although the production was intelligently directed, its almost slavish obedience to representing the history that explains the play made the production seem rather like a museum piece.

1987   In his production for the Royal Shakespeare Company in Stratford, Jonathan Miller again experimented with a historical interpretation of the play: the program for this production emphasized the masculine-centered, hierarchical understanding of political and family life in the period in which the play was written. This time around, however, Miller used history as a backdrop against which he explored Katherina's psychology in distinctly modern terms—

Fiona Shaw played the character with a number of idiosyncrasies that suggested a neurotic response to her oppressive family conditions.

1990   In a touring production for the Royal Shakespeare Company that played in Stratford during the 1992 season, Bill Alexander adapted the framing plot to portray the Lord and his friends as snobbish upper-class Sloane-ranger types who set out to teach Sly a lesson. The shrewish Katherina's lesson in humility served instead as an example for the boorish young aristocrats.

1994   Gale Edwards's production for the Royal Shakespeare Company imagined the Lord of the Induction as a dream master who literally conjured up a dream of male domination for Sly. In homage to Bogdanov's 1978 production, Edward's Lord conjured Sly's wife to play Katherina, who was degraded and forced into submission by Sly/Petruchio.

1999   Gil Junger's film *10 Things I Hate About You* adapted Shakespeare's play to a contemporary American high school setting. Fascinating as a study of recent attitudes toward feminism, the film interpreted Kat's shrewishness as feminist resistance to men that she must ultimately leave behind. Its insights about sexuality and gender bear little relation to Shakespeare's. (See Inspired by *The Taming of the Shrew*.)

2003   Gregory Doran staged *The Taming of the Shrew* in the Royal Shakespeare Theatre and John Fletcher's *The Woman's Prize* in the Swan Theatre at Stratford. The production of Shakespeare's play explored Katherina's dysfunctional social environment and debilitating self-doubt as well as Petruchio's childish insecurities about his father's death to explain the characters' tempestuous wooing and marriage. These same problems reflected on Petruchio in Fletcher's play. Doran's was the first staging of Fletcher's play by a major company since the eighteenth century, and apparently the first time both plays had been staged in conjunction since they were performed at the court of Charles I in 1633.

2005   Coming full circle from Shakespeare's all-male theater, an all-woman acting troupe, the Queen's Company, staged *The Taming of the Shrew* in New York City. Director Rebecca Patterson focused on the emotional openness of characters of both genders, but in attempting to reclaim this apparently misogynist play for women's voices, Patterson stressed Katherina's pivotal role in a dynamic relationship with Petruchio.

Inspired by *The Taming of the Shrew*

The story of Katherina Minola's taming has fallen in and out of fashion since Shakespeare's play first debuted in the early 1590s. Today, *The Shrew*'s depiction of the repeated, often cruel humiliations levied against an unhappily married woman makes many readers uncomfortable or angry. However, Shakespeare himself does not insist on the perfect justice or the perfect success of Petruchio's wife-taming methods. The open-ended nature of the play—the fact that it allows us to dwell on the question of whether the shrew has actually been tamed, whether she deserved to be tamed, and why one might go about such a thing as "taming" another individual in the first place—has allowed later artists and authors to weigh in with their own opinions. Most adaptations of *The Taming of the Shrew* focus on the issue of power relations between the sexes. The play's framing text about the adventures of the drunken tinker, Christopher Sly, has also contributed significantly to the play's literary afterlife, often becoming enmeshed in larger discussions about the dynamics between men and women as well as between the powerful and the weak.

Stage

The first full-length adaptation of *The Taming of the Shrew* dates to 1611, when the aspiring London playwright John Fletcher produced his comedy *The Woman's Prize; or, The Tamer Tamed*. Fletcher's play, conceived as a sequel to Shakespeare's, begins after Katherina has died and Petruchio has remarried. *The Woman's Prize* chronicles the efforts of Maria, Petruchio's modern-minded second wife, to turn the tables on her famously dominant spouse. In response to Maria's defiance, Petruchio rages, feigns sickness, determines to take to sea, and finally tries the most foolproof method available for attracting pity: he plays dead. His witty wife is not deceived, however, and the play concludes with the couple reconciling and Petruchio tacitly promising to honor and obey Maria's wishes for the rest of his life. The myth of Shakespeare's *Shrew*—that a woman can ever be completely tamed—is laid to rest by Fletcher's boisterous, irreverent comedy.

The next major stage work based on *The Shrew* is a Restoration play entitled *Sauny the Scot: or, The Taming of the Shrew*. Composed by the author and actor John Lacy, the comedy was first performed during the late 1660s. Lacy altered the conclusion of Shakespeare's play to caricature the shrew's resistance to her husband. His shrew, Margaret, works herself into a double bind when she swears never to speak again after Petruchio compliments her on the eloquence of her insults. The ludicrous and menacing Sauny, Petruchio's Scottish man-servant (a role invented and played by Lacy himself), made a particular impression on audiences of the day. Sauny is dirty, belligerent, crude, and quick to anger, thereby demonstrating several seventeenth-century anti-Scottish stereotypes. At the same time, however, he proves instrumental to Petruchio's domination of Margaret, and Petruchio seems glad to make use of him. The way in which Sauny manhandles and intimidates his master's rebellious wife into obedience makes it clear to the audience that Petruchio's taming of Margaret represents an act of violent usurpation.

For a time after Lacy's play there seems to have been a strong literary association between *The Taming of the Shrew* and all things Scottish. In 1716, two London authors wrote brief farces based on the

Christopher Sly subplot in *The Shrew*. One author, Charles Johnson, had recent politics in mind. In 1715, a rebellion in Scotland had alarmed much of England. The rising was in support of the "Old Pretender," James Francis Edward Stewart, whose claim to the throne rivaled that of the English monarch George I. Charles Johnson's *Cobler of Preston* transforms Christopher Sly from a man of few words to a hot-tempered country cobbler who likes to mix his drink with traitorous toasts to the health of the Pretender. Johnson's farce turns Shakespeare's meditation on correct relations between men and women into an examination of correct relations between men and their government. When a local gentleman, Sir Charles, picks up the drunken Sly from the gutter and transforms him briefly into a "lord," the cobbler's temporary delusions of social grandeur mirror his deluded belief in the false claims of the Pretender. When Sir Charles arranges for a group of men masquerading as state police to surprise Christopher with accusations of treason, the cobbler quickly sobers up and repents.

The introduction of Christopher Bullock's short entertainment, also performed in 1716 and also called *The Cobler of Preston*, mocks Charles Johnson's farce for its political pretensions. Bullock's version of the Christopher Sly story is a simple comedic tale. Sly (renamed Toby Guzzle) is given an outspoken wife, Dorcas Guzzle, whose objection to his drinking habits—and his tendency to spend long hours in the company of the ale-wife Cicely Hacket—provides the main interest of the plot. When the local lord plays the identity trick on Toby Guzzle, convincing him that he is an aristocrat with the legal power to punish local wrongdoers, Guzzle tries to tame Dorcas and Cicely and orders that they be dunked in the river for disorderly conduct. When he returns to his true life as a poor cobbler, he finds himself confronted with two wet and angry women. A short brawl ensues, followed by a quickly patched-up peace. Bullock's entertainment not only insists that we leave politics out of the theater; it also suggests that we shouldn't believe that either sex could ever emerge as the dominant force within a marriage.

The later eighteenth century saw two further adaptations of *The Taming of the Shrew*. James Wordale's *A Cure for a Scold* (1735) is a brief "ballad farce" that combines songs with dialogue mostly derived from Lacy's *Sauny the Scot*. In 1754, the legendary actor and author David Garrick produced his own adaptation of *The Taming of the Shrew*. This version, entitled *Catharine and Petruchio*, went on to dominate the stage until the mid-nineteenth century. Garrick's play condenses the action to three acts and focuses on the interaction between the title characters. Christopher Sly disappears, as does the subplot concerning the marriage of Katherina's sister Bianca. Garrick's play is meant as a star vehicle, designed to showcase the abilities of popular actors and actresses. Its stage directions firmly establish particular dramatic conventions for the play, including physical struggles between the bickering couple, whose battle of wits has produced a long accompanying history of choreographed stage fights. *Catharine and Petruchio* ends on a definitive note, with Petruchio firmly in control of both events and his own marriage. Audiences seem to have found this pleasing.

After the eighteenth century, further revisions of *The Taming of the Shrew* did not appear until the mid-twentieth century. Cole Porter's famous 1948 musical *Kiss Me, Kate* stays true to the double plot of the original Shakespeare play. This time, however, the follies of Christopher Sly are replaced by the follies of a divorced theater couple, Lilli Vanessi and Fred Graham, who have decided to join forces professionally one final time in a musical production of *The Taming of the Shrew*. Vanessi and Graham play the feuding lovers Kate and Petruchio, but matters are complicated by Graham's flirtation with the seductive Lois Lane, who plays Bianca. The Porter musical turns the conflict between the principal actors into a humorous, comical battle. Since both "Kate" and "Petruchio" obviously suffer from artistic temperaments and a shared love of melodrama, *Kiss Me, Kate* takes the nasty edge off the repeated physical tussles between Vanessi and Graham, bringing the plot firmly back within the realm of light-hearted farce.

Charles Marowitz's version of *The Taming of the Shrew*, first performed in 1975, goes for the precise opposite effect. Marowitz's production represents Petruchio's courtship of Katherina as a sadistic exercise in brainwashing. Starved, terrorized, and deprived of sleep by her psychotic bridegroom, Katherina falls into a trance. In her dream, she imagines that she has been returned to the safety of her family home and her unmarried life. Katherina can hardly believe this luxurious vision, and Marowitz creates a poignant effect by having her speak the same lines Christopher Sly utters when he awakens as a supposed lord: "[D]o I dream? Or have I dreamed till now? / I do not sleep: I see, I hear, I speak. / I smell sweet savors and I feel soft things." Like Sly's dream, however, Katherina's is not destined to endure. Marowitz's version stages her final speech about wifely duty as the rote recitation of a broken woman, destroyed by a cabal of violent men.

Film and Television

John Ford's romantic comedy *The Quiet Man* (1952) is perhaps the best-regarded film adaptation of *The Taming of the Shrew*. John Wayne stars as Sean Thornton, an Irish-American boxer who has decided to retire in the land of his ancestors. Maureen O'Hara plays Mary Kate Danaher, a beautiful firebrand who catches Thornton's eye as soon as he sets foot in his home village of Innisfree. Ford's film builds on plot elements of *The Shrew* that emphasize the communal effort to change Katherina's behavior. Sean does not tame his bride alone: he has the assistance of Mary Kate's family and he draws on a clear set of social expectations regarding proper wifely behavior. After some heated bantering, Sean proposes to Mary Kate, and she accepts. However, Mary Kate's volatile brother, Will Danaher, refuses to pay his sister's dowry. Sean accepts this loss, but Mary Kate cannot. According to her system of values, a woman without a dowry is literally worthless, and she sees her brother's refusal to pay as a strike against the marriage as well as a public shame. When the feud with Will turns into a marital feud, setting Thornton and Mary Kate at bitter odds during the first days of their wedded life, the new husband quickly learns that in a romantic partnership, what is important to one partner is of necessity important to both. The ex-boxer must come out of retirement to correct his own image in the eyes of the villagers and thereby in the eyes of his wife. Thus, Ford inverts the plot of the Shakespearean play: whereas the Katherina of *The Shrew* must become calmer and gentler to achieve social acceptance, the "Petruchio" of *The Quiet Man* must acquire a local reputation for fierceness before he can realize his dream of a peaceful life.

Modern audiences have been most comfortable with adaptations that place the balance of power in the woman's hands. For instance, the next adaptation of *The Shrew* appears in the popular TV series *Moonlighting* (1985–1989), where the main male character, David Addison, is the employee of the main female character, Maddie Hayes. He runs the Blue Moon detective agency, but she owns and directs the company. Fireworks erupt as the two become increasingly invested in the business and romantically interested in, but also infuriated by, each other. In a highly popular 1986 episode entitled "Atomic Shakespeare," a young boy reading *The Taming of the Shrew* for a class assignment imagines the characters of his favorite show, *Moonlighting*, performing the roles in Shakespeare's play. When Petruchio/David marries Katherina/Maddie against her will, he admonishes, "Thou art my goods, my property, my stuff!" She promptly replies, "Stuff your stuff!" The newlyweds bicker throughout the episode, but eventually both husband and wife are tamed by their growing affection and respect for one another. At a feast at Katherina's father's house, Petruchio orders Katherina to call the sun the moon, just as Shakespeare's Petruchio does in Act Four, scene five. Katherina insists that her husband has made a mistake and asks him to look again. Petruchio does, admits his error, and then announces to the entire assembly that he renounces the dowry he had been promised if he managed to tame Katherina, since he wishes from his wife "no other reward other than thy affection, and thy company for as long as thee shall live."

In 1999, Gil Junger's *10 Things I Hate About You* mapped the plot of Shakespeare's play onto a modern-day California high school, Padua High. Katherina becomes Katarina Stratford, a fierce and socially isolated senior who can't wait to break free from sunny Padua and start studying feminist literature at a small liberal arts college on the East Coast. Her Petruchio, Patrick Verona, is a similarly isolated individual, a loner with a bad reputation for violent stunts and anti-social behavior. But Kat Stratford is only to be won with kindness. So far from starving, beating, or shaming her, Patrick quits smoking and feigns an interest in the bands Katarina likes to get her to take him seriously. By the end of the film, the bad boy loner has been revealed as a steady and respectful partner for the smart, volatile woman his attentions have finally earned. In a similar vein, the 2003 romantic comedy *Deliver Us from Eva* shows the film's Petruchio, Kay, drawn both to the beauty and the independent spirit of his Katherina, Eva. Interestingly, both of these recent films conclude with a scene in which "Petruchio" must ask forgiveness for his past behavior to secure his leading lady's future affection. In the late twentieth and early twenty-first centuries, it seems that any reference to the taming of unruly women necessitates a gesture of apology and contrition—from male film characters, directors, and screenwriters alike.

Dance and Music

Although *The Taming of the Shrew* has not been adapted often for the ballet, it does boast one particularly successful, comedic version. The Stuttgart Ballet production, choreographed by John Cranko to music by Kurt-Heinz Stolze, was first seen in 1969 and has remained an audience favorite ever since. Cranko's choreography highlights the rough-and-tumble nature of Katherina and Petruchio's early encounters and skillfully demonstrates how the pair's relationship shifts into mutual cooperation and trust via their collaboration in dance.

Opera composers have periodically attempted *The Shrew*, beginning in the nineteenth century when the Romantic vogue for Shakespeare first began to take hold. Hermann Goetz's production was first performed in 1874. It appears to have been a creditable musical attempt, strongly influenced by Schumann, but did not make it into the rotation of regularly performed operas. Likewise, Vittorio Giannini's 1953 *Taming of the Shrew* did not find sufficient favor with audiences and critics to become a staple of the operatic world. In 1957, the Soviet composer Vissarion Shebalin wrote the best regarded opera score to date. Shebalin was a traditionalist who drew on the work of Tchaikovsky and Prokofiev. His finely drawn and somewhat musically conservative version remains the critic's choice, although, again, it is rarely performed.

Sly, a 1927 opera by the German Italian composer Ermanno Wolf-Ferrari, has recently been revived at the Washington Opera (1999) and the Metropolitan Opera (2002). The protagonist of the opera is Christopher Sly, rewritten as a destitute poet pursued by creditors. When he stumbles into the temporary safe haven of a London tavern, he drinks too much and is taken up by the Earl of Westmoreland, who decides to play the traditional Shakespearean identity trick on him. Wolf-Ferrari's opera swerves into tragedy, however, when Sly falls in love with Dolly, the earl's mistress, who has been assigned to play his wife. Dolly returns Sly's affections, but he only learns this after he has been cast back into his old life and deprived of her. Sly's aristocratic adventure ends in the despairing poet's suicide. Wolf-Ferrari's opera, turning from Katherina and Petruchio to examine the ethical issues inherent in *The Taming of the Shrew*'s framing text, condemns the frivolous intervention of the powerful in the lives of the weak.

For Further Reading
by Nicholas F. Radel

Boose, Lynda E. "Scolding Brides and Bridling Scolds: Taming the Woman's Unruly Member." *Shakespeare Quarterly* 42 (Summer 1991): 179–213. Boose provides detailed evidence about the various disciplinary rituals used to define a woman's place in the early modern social order to show how Katherina's taming constitutes a rehearsal of predominant power relations.

Burns, Margie. "The Ending of *The Shrew*." *Shakespeare Studies* 18 (1986): 41–64.Burns reads the possibilities for individual transformation explored in the deliberately unfinished Induction tale as a key to understanding the humane values in the conclusion of the taming plot.

Crocker, Holly A. "Affective Resistance: Performing Passivity and Playing A-Part in *The Taming of the Shrew*." *Shakespeare Quarterly* 54 (Summer 2003): 142–159.Beginning with a theorized view of gender, Crocker shows how Katherina's paradoxical embrace of feminine passivity in the final moments of the play blurs the power distinctions Petruchio works to create.

Detmer, Emily. "Civilizing Subordination: Domestic Violence and *The Taming of the Shrew*." *Shakespeare Quarterly* 48 (Fall 1997): 273–294. Reacting against readings of the taming plot as farce or a mutual game played between matched partners, Detmer argues that in an era when physical violence was increasingly eschewed as a means of spousal control, *The Shrew* acted as a roadmap for newer psychological forms of domination.

Dolan, Fran. "Marriage" and "The Household." In *The Taming of the Shrew: Texts and Contexts*, 160–243. Boston: Bedford/St. Martin's, 1996. Two chapters in Dolan's edition for the *Text and Context* series provide compelling historical overviews of ideas about marriage and household authority in Shakespeare's era, as well as reprints of the highly significant historical sources from which she draws her ideas.

Fineman, Joel. "The Turn of the Shrew." In *Shakespeare and the Question of Theory*, edited by Patricia Parker and Geoffrey Hartman, 138–159. New York: Methuen, 1985. In a difficult but important article, Fineman argues that the indeterminate, rhetorical language of the word games both Katherina and Petruchio play represent the subversive other of the play's attempt to render meaning determinate.

Haring-Smith, Tori. *From Farce to Melodrama: A Stage History of* The Taming of the Shrew, *1594–1983*. Contributions in Drama and Theatre Studies, no. 16. Westport, CT: Greenwood Press, 1985. An indispensible guide to productions over several centuries, Haring-Smith's book also provides an account of the network of interpretive traditions that developed among those productions.

Korda, Natasha. "Household Kates: Domesticating Commodities in *The Taming of the Shrew.*" *Shakespeare Quarterly* 47 (Summer 1996): 109–131. Korda relates Petruchio's taming of Katherina to the new domestic roles early modern women were beginning to play as consumers in a nascent capitalist economy.

Mangan, Michael. "Anxiety and Dominance: Petruccio, Patriarchy, *Patriarcha.*" In *Staging Masculinities: History, Gender, Performance,* 61–69. Basingstoke, Hampshire, UK: Palgrave Macmillan, 2003. In a short subchapter, Mangan argues that Petruchio's masculinity can be understood in terms of his conflating two commedia dell'arte roles, the lover and the braggart soldier.

Marcus, Leah. "The Shakespearean Editor as Shrew-Tamer." *English Literary Renaissance* 22 (1992): 177–200. Demonstrating that critics' and editors' interpretations of the relationship between the anonymous play *The Taming of a Shrew* and Shakespeare's *The Taming of the Shrew* have been shaped by historical changes in expectations about women, Marcus provides a useful analysis of the relative merits of the two plays.

Maurer, Margaret. "Constering Bianca: *The Taming of the Shrew* and *The Woman's Prize; or The Tamer Tamed.*" *Medieval and Renaissance Drama in England* 14 (2001): 186–206. Highly useful as a comparison of Shakespeare's play to Fletcher's *The Woman's Prize*, Maurer's essay is also a fascinating study of the editorial emendations that, she argues, obscure the subversive role Bianca plays in the Folio text of *The Shrew.*

Moisan, Thomas. "'What's that to you?' or Facing Facts: Anti-Paternalist Chords and Social Discords in *The Taming of the Shrew.*" *Renaissance Drama* 26 (1995): 105–129. Moisan argues that *The Shrew* resists patriarchal values and authority by showing that the social and familial discord Petruchio introduces into the play is not satisfactorily resolved by its conclusion.

Newman, Karen. "Renaissance Family Politics and Shakespeare's *Taming of the Shrew*." In *Fashioning Femininity and English Renaissance Drama*, 33–50. Chicago: University of Chicago Press, 1991. Exploring the play in relation to historical discourses that see women's independent appropriation of language as a threat to patriarchal authority, Newman argues that the play itself can only present an imaginary, formal solution to the larger social contradictions it embodies.

Novy, Marianne. "Patriarchy and Play in *The Taming of the Shrew*." *English Literary Renaissance* 9 (1979): 264–280. Novy's essay represents one important strand of thinking about the meaning of *The Shrew*: the taming of Katherina is a series of verbal games Petruchio teaches Katherina to play so that she might learn to reconcile herself to the limitations of the patriarchal society in which they both live.

Seronsy, Cecil C. "'Supposes' as the Unifying Theme in *The Taming of the Shrew*." *Shakespeare Quarterly* 14 (Winter 1963): 15–30. A classic account of the relationship between the Bianca/Lucentio subplot and the taming plot of *The Shrew*. Seronsy shows how Shakespeare achieved thematic unity by enlarging on the themes of pretending and disguise that he adopted from his major source, Gascoigne's play *The Supposes*.

Sloan, LaRue Love. " 'Caparisoned like the horse': Tongue and Tail in Shakespeare's *The Taming of the Shrew*." *Early Modern Literary Studies* 10.2 (September 2004): 1.1–24. Sloan provides a detailed reading of Biondello's speech at 3.2.41–60 as a parody of the infamous skimmington ride.

Underdown, David. "The Taming of the Scold: The Enforcement of Patriarchal Authority in Early Modern England." In *Order and Disorder in Early Modern England,* edited by Anthony Fletcher and John Stevenson, 116–136. Cambridge: Cambridge University Press, 1985. Underdown, a historian, links Shakespeare's play to social and cultural tensions brought about by a seeming increase in incidents of unruly female behavior that accompanied the emergence of capitalism in early modern English towns and woodlands.

Wayne, Valerie. "Refashioning the Shrew." *Shakespeare Studies* 17 (1985): 159–187. Locating *The Shrew* within a network of plays by the medieval Wakefield Master and Shakespeare himself, Wayne shows that Katherina is not simply a socially disruptive figure but also a creative one.

Wentersdorf, Karl P. "The Original Ending of *The Taming of the Shrew*: A Reconsideration." *Studies in English Literature* 18 (1978): 201–215. Addressing the question of the apparently unfinished Induction from a dramatic rather than a thematic angle, Wentersdorf provides evidence from the Folio text that the Induction was completed at some point during composition.